# Headwinds

## The Dead Reckoning of the Heart

Thomas A. Reis

authorHOUSE®

*AuthorHouse™ LLC*
*1663 Liberty Drive*
*Bloomington, IN 47403*
*www.authorhouse.com*
*Phone: 1-800-839-8640*

*Published by AuthorHouse 07/30/2014*

*ISBN: 978-1-4918-1952-4 (sc)*
*ISBN: 978-1-4918-1953-1 (hc)*
*ISBN: 978-1-4918-1954-8 (e)*

*Library of Congress Control Number: 2013917182*

*This book is printed on acid-free paper.*

To "G", the most loving, caring, sensitive soul I've ever known. Without you and your guidance, none of this would exist.

# Acknowledgements

My thanks go out to the following people for their help with *Headwinds: The Dead Reckoning of the Heart.*

To my first editors, my sister, Mary Lark, and my forever "sister-in-law," Mary Cook, who painstakingly went through each page of my manuscript correcting all spelling and grammatical errors.

To my colleague Dave Page, who also provided me with initial editorial help that gave me a glimmer of hope in seeing this through to publication.

To my primary editor, Dr. Laura Markos, who through her patience, dedication, and hard work made the dream of publication go from a fantasy to reality. Without you, none of this would be. I'm so grateful and appreciative of your work.

To Karen Stansberry at AuthorHouse, who believed in my story, supported me along my journey, and had faith in the transcendence of my story. Thank you for believing in a first-time author.

To my sister Lilly Doerfler, who has always been my biggest fan, who was the first person to listen to me read my manuscript to her from start to finish, and believed in the story. Thank you for all your encouragement and love.

To Soulaire Ailerai, who introduced me to "G" and became a lifelong friend along the way. Thanks for always believing in me. I've always got your back.

And finally, to my mentors for life, Eileen "Gramma" Lund and Tony Jurich. To Gramma, who taught us to "love many and each the most," thank you for always believing in me, my "Mom of choice." And to Tony, my academic father, uncle, and brother, who left this world way too soon, a part of you is in everything I do. Thank you. I so miss you!

*The deep parts of my life pour onward,*
*as if the river shores were opening out.*
*It seems that things are more like me now,*
*that I can see farther into paintings.*
*I feel closer to what language can't reach.*

– Ranier Marie Rilke

### ***NOTE TO THE READER***

Some of the names of people and places have been changed to protect the innocent.

# The Letter

Christmas was approaching. I was in graduate school earning my MSW at the University of Georgia. My parents asked what I wanted for Christmas. I didn't want another sweater or shirt or pair of jeans. And then, after a pause, this idea came to me:

> *I'd like you to each write a letter to me. Write it as if it is the last letter you would ever send to me. The rule is that you can't consult each other on it. That's all I want for Christmas; each of you writes me letters as if it was the last I would ever hear from you. What would you want to say?*

My mom, not surprisingly, wrote in her letter about finding Jesus and staying close to the Lord. But this is part of what my father wrote, which has stayed with me ever since:

*Christmas, 1983*

*Dear Tom,*

> *Well, this is a most unusual request; for your Christmas present, you wanted me to write you a letter (without talking to your mother about it) and write it as if it was the last letter I ever wrote to you. What would I say to my son if this was it? I'm 62 years old as I sit down to write*

*this; let's hope there are many more years ahead before this truly is the case! Geez, where do I begin?*

*Actually, I've got to tell you that I have been pondering this for some time ever since you made the request over a month ago. Where would I start . . . . I've started this a dozen times and hardly get beyond "Dear Tom" before I find myself crumpling up another sheet of paper. Each time I sit down to write, I draw a blank. How do I tell you something I've never told you before? I've got so many things to say but how do I say it? Where do I begin? Maybe I'll start at the beginning . . . your birth.*

*I know, you hear about your birth story as each one of your birthdays pass, by because your mother replays the whole ordeal in "living color" to "celebrate" the occasion in the re-telling of the tale. Since your mother is such a great story teller, I always let her take the lead as she regales us with the annual story of your birth. God knows I've never been much of a story teller! I'm not sure why I never told you my side of the story; perhaps I was always waiting for the "right time" or when you became a man. But now you are 25 years old, in graduate school, and for some reason, now seems like the right time to tell you, so here goes.*

*When your mother's time was due we called the ambulance and in 3 minutes flat they were at the door. Soon we were racing down the freeway toward Chicago and Little Company of Mary Hospital at 85 mph when I heard the attendant say, "Her water broke!" Minutes later, as they backed into the emergency entrance of the hospital, and peeled back the blanket that covered your mother, I heard the attendant then say, "Like hell that's water, its blood!" Apparently your mother's placenta had burst on the ride in. Soon your mother was whisked away in a stretcher as I was directed in to the Expectant Father's Room.*

*I paced back and forth in that room for about an hour when the doctor came in to apprise me of the situation.*

*"Your wife was touch and go for a while but I think we can save her; I think she's going to make it. But your son is another story; I'm not sure he is going to make it." He paused and then added, "It may not be a bad idea to just let him go; he has a birth defect hand (none of the digits are fully formed) and his face is all deformed. It would not surprise me if he has extensive brain damage as well. I'm thinking it might be better for his quality of life and yours if we just let him go and concentrate on saving your wife."*

*I paused for a moment as the reality of his words sunk in . . . "brain damaged," "birth defect," "deformity" . . . . My head began to spin with all kinds of thoughts, and then I felt a rage well up inside of me, like I was watching a scene from a movie unfold before me; I found the words pouring out of my mouth coming from a place deep within me, a place I was not familiar with; I shouted "He has every right to live and you will do everything you can to save him. I want to see him right now!" Later I found myself looking through a glass box at you with all kinds of tubes connected to you to keep you alive and I thought how easy it would have been to turn the oxygen flow off the respirator and let you die. For some reason in that moment of standing over you, it must have been the hand of God, I all of a sudden felt great peace, I knew you would make it . . . .*

I never heard my father's side of the story until that moment almost 30 years ago when I first read those words. It shook me to the core. It dawned on me that I owe my life to the decision my father made in that moment, in that waiting room long ago. This man, who was always in the background, always a mystery to me, a man who never said much, never shared much, when it came time to step up, he did, he said yes to my life. And for that I am grateful.

I have often pondered what that moment must have been like for him. Bringing a crippled baby into the world in the 1950s was very different from today. It was not unusual at that time for parents and doctors to collude and let kids born with disabilities die rather than to live a life destined for multiple hospitalizations and institutionalization. The United States, and for that matter the world, wasn't a very accepting place for disabilities. The quality of life was not very good at all for the disabled at that time. People with disabilities were frequently segregated in institutions away from the public, and the idea of educating and employing them wasn't a part of our collective imagination back then.

And then I think about the desperation my father surely must have felt as the sole breadwinner of our family. He was working two full-time jobs to put food on the table and pay the mortgage, living paycheck to paycheck, with three kids under 5 years old. He almost loses the mother of his children and the love of his life and then he is told that his fourth child, his youngest, is severely handicapped and may be brain damaged. I often wonder if I would have made the same choice if I were in his shoes. Would I have followed the doctor's advice and pulled the plug? Was the tougher choice to let me live?

Thus began the story of my life.

# A World of Difference

### THE STARE

*I've seen that look if not*
*a million times before.*
*Oh, it's changed over the years ~*
*people seem to hide it better as they*
*grow older, The Stare.*
*It's a stare that boxes me*
*into a fate*
*I cannot change.*
*A box that seems forever*
*to remain the same.*
*Please tell me if this really is*
*some kind of a game.*
*I may look different but*
*our hearts beat the same ~*
*I may need more assistance*
*but I'm not immune to pain.*
*Oh, please, once, just show me*
*that you care ~ I care.*
*My questions of why echo on*
*inside,*
*the answer seems ever distant*
*as I wait for a reply.*
*Don't get too close, don't spend too*

*much time.*
*Don't touch, don't share, no one*
*ever dares.*
*The stare comes back ~ it always*
*does, but seldom does*
*it care.*
*It follows me wherever I roam,*
*a stare that does not dare ask*
*me "why"?*
*A stare I see forever, inside.*
-- Thomas A. Reis, 1982

Amazing how decisions made in the moment, decisions made with little thought of consequence, can have effects that last a lifetime.

The last words my mother heard before losing consciousness that night were, "If we can't save both of them, then we go for neither of them."

Thus ended my mother's life. My mother "died" for 3 or 4 minutes; she has never forgotten that moment. She remembers slowly leaving her body and watching nine nurses and doctors frantically trying to resuscitate her dying body. Over to the side, I was on another table surrounded by my own set of nurses and doctors trying to keep me alive as well.

She remembers moving to a great, white, penetrating light and the feeling of peace like a curtain being drawn over her, feeling a sense of warmth and connection that she had never felt before or since. She was basking in this surreal space between this world and the next, and in an instant, like someone switching on a bright light in a dark room, she remembers being back in her body. She rebelled at the thought of being back as her body convulsed in pain, but she has never forgotten those moments spent suspended out of her body. That was my mom's near death experience, and that was the start of my life.

The evening started out innocently enough. It was late at night and a rare moment of rest when my mom was watching the weekly

Western series called *Gunsmoke* at the end of yet another evening caring for my three other siblings, all under 5 years old. That's when the first pains started. They were annoying and spaced far enough apart yet, like background noise, ever present.

My brother and sisters were all sleeping and Dad was sleeping as well, having just finished his second job, another 16+ hour day. The house was quiet with just the flickering of the black and white TV and the dim light on next to the Lazy Boy. My mom was sitting in it with her feet propped up, resting her tired legs.

The pain intensified. Flo, the neighbor behind us who was a good friend of my mother's, saw the light on through the kitchen window, as she frequently did, to visit with my mom late at night. Mom was frequently up at all hours with one child or another, taking care of innumerable ailments. It became a regular occurrence for Flo to come over and help out.

The pains now were gaining intensity. Still, Mom hesitated, not wanting to wake my father, who was tired and exhausted. Sleep was a rare commodity for my father in those days. Eventually, the pain became so great she awoke my dad.

After assurances that Flo would stay back with the kids, my mom and dad found themselves in the back of an ambulance speeding the 20+ miles to Little Company of Mary hospital on the south side of Chicago.

In order to save my life, and with my mother "dying," the doctors used forceps to pull me out of her belly quickly. In using forceps, however, they put too much pressure on my right temple region and cut off the facial nerve, leaving me with a palsy paralysis on the right side of my face, causing permanent muscle and nerve damage. The result is a permanently crooked smile and an asymmetrical face, causing unimaginable pain that would become a reservoir of personal despair. Along with a crooked smile, I would have a deformed lip, my right eye constantly drips tears from the strain of never being able to fully close, and one eye would be more open than the other.

As if my face wasn't enough of a challenge, I was also born with a birth defect left hand I have always referred to as "Nubby." When

I was 3 years old, I asked my mom, "Why did I get Nubby?" She had a load of laundry in one hand and was taking out the garbage with the other, but my question stopped her in her tracks. She thought for a moment and then, looking down on me, she replied, "I just didn't have enough," and then walked out of the room.

All these years later, it made sense that she "didn't have enough." After all, she had four kids in 4½ years, I was the last born, and she was all of 5' 2" and under 109 pounds when she gave birth to me, on top of which she smoked—facts that I'm sure went a lot further in explaining why I live with Nubby today. I never have brought any of this knowledge to her attention, since I'm sure on some level she blames herself for the way I look. Why place even more of a burden on her conscience?

I always liked the term *Nubby*. I always thought it was kind of cute. About 20 years ago, when I was first married to my former wife, out of concern that Nubby might be genetic, we went through genetic counseling. I found out Nubby's scientific name was *terminal transfer defect*; I liked Nubby a whole lot better. Terminal transfer defect sounded like a disease—way too scientific sounding! I did find out it occurs early in fetal development and it is predominant in males. Frequently over the years, people would ask me if I was a thalidomide baby. A drug frequently prescribed for pregnant mothers in the 1950s, outside of showing up at U.S. military bases overseas and in Canada, thalidomide was never an approved drug in the U.S. So my answer was always, "No, I am not a thalidomide baby."

And so my entry in to the world was anything but normal. I was not only born with a birth defect hand and a paralysis of the right side of my face, but I was also born with asthma. My mother would start out every morning in my life during that first year washing down all the dust from the ceiling, the floor, and all four walls of my bedroom in order to help my struggling breathing.

On three different occasions during my first year, I was given the last rites, and my parents along with the nurses stood around my bed waiting for me to take my last breath. But for some reason, I didn't die. (When I used to recall this story later on in my life, I would tell people that I was like a roach; no matter what happened, I just wouldn't die). My mother's constant prayer was, "Please, God, if my son is going to be a bad person, if he is going to do harm to the world, please take him now. But if he is going to be a good person, if he is going to make a difference in this world, then please, let him live." I often think back at that little prayer and wonder, that's one hell of a thought to fulfill!

I often wondered over the years how things could have been different. What if my mom did have proper prenatal nutrition and hadn't weighed less than 109 pounds at my birth? What if she hadn't smoked during her pregnancy? What if she hadn't waited so long to tell my father? What if they had stopped at one of the seven hospitals they passed on their way to their doctor's hospital over 20 miles away? Of course, I never bring up any of these questions with them; what's the use? It doesn't change anything. The questions never come up with them either, or least they don't voice them in my presence. Still, the questions linger.

It is like I tell my students at the college where I teach: Life is like a card game. Sometimes you are dealt a great hand, and other times you don't like the cards. You can moan and groan and yell that it isn't fair, but in the end, no matter how crummy the hand that you are holding, it becomes your responsibility to play out that hand as best you can. No one else can play the hand for you. When it is your life, there is not a lot of room for bluffing.

When I was 4 years old, I came down with pneumonia and was hospitalized for 2 weeks in an oxygen tent. My first time away from home, I was scared and lonely. It didn't help that at night, when visiting hours were over, I would be awakened and wheeled away by nurses and doctors to a back room on another floor. They would attach electrodes on my face and then experiment on me by sending various levels of shock to my face. I would then indicate if I could feel a shock or if it was greater than before. They would keep shocking me with electrical current running through my face, continually asking, "Do you feel that? Do you feel that?" I kept wondering, "Why are they doing this to me? Where are my parents?" It is 54 years later as I write these words, and I'm still very averse to any overhead, bright, halogen lights shining in my presence today, like they did all those nights when hospital personnel experimented on me. Only after I told my parents, about 7 days into my stay there, did the experiments stop. This happened in 1962. Before the Americans with Disability Act took effect in 1975, it was not unusual for people with disabilities to be experimented on without parental or patient consent.

I always liked Halloween as a kid. It had to be one of the best days of the year. On Halloween, I could put on a mask and, for one day a year, I could fit in like everyone else. In my costume I didn't stick out anymore. No one could see I was different. No one stared back at me. For one day in the year, I could just blend in and be normal. No one would be whispering to a friend. I wasn't poked fun at, taunted, or laughed at. I could just be Casper the Ghost—almost invisible.

People with disabilities are used to sticking out, and being unique. It really is ironic because the able bodied want to feel special, beautiful, and unique. They want to stand out in some way—for their good looks, their charm, or their personality. People born with a disability stand out their whole lives, but for all the wrong reasons. They've stood out not because they are beautiful, but because they are different. And one of the earliest lessons I learned with my disability is that difference doesn't equal beautiful.

I never knew I was different until I started going to school. As I was growing up, my parents always told me, "Tommy, you're a beautiful boy." I was told that I was no different from anyone else, and I believed it.

My disability was never allowed to be used as an excuse. The word *can't* wasn't allowed in my vocabulary. When difficulties arose regarding my disability, my parents would tell me, "I guess you have decided you won't be doing that," rather than allowing me to say, "I can't do" whatever. I was always told, by my mom especially, that I could do "anything I set my mind to." Others in my family took their cue from my mom and believed it to be true.

So with great shock, I found out that things were different when I left the cocoon of my family's love and entered the world of school. It was there, in kindergarten that I discovered that I was very different and that difference wasn't something to celebrate. Difference was something to be ridiculed, hated, and looked down upon.

Frequently in those first years of school, kids would gather in groups of three or four in the corner and quietly whisper to one another, pointing discreetly to my hand and face. They would glance at me and giggle amongst themselves, never making any eye contact. Slowly, one by one, they would leave the group and approach me cautiously, trying to locate my little hand and take a closer look at my deformed face.

It happened so often that I would make it harder for them. I would hide Nubby in my pocket. Sometimes when their staring became so blatant, as they approached I would surprise them and stare right back at them saying, "What are you looking at?"

As their frustration grew, they became bolder and bolder. They would come up to me in pairs and groups and crinkle up their one hand so that it resembled Nubby. Then with their other hand, they would crinkle their faces and make them look crooked like mine, and proceed to taunt and poke fun at me. To this day, as an adult, I never remember teachers ever intervening much on my behalf. Instead, I would take it and take it until I could take no more and I began fighting back. I tried to ignore their harsh ridicule. But when it became unbearable, and I began to lash out and fight back.

At night before going to bed, I would kneel at the foot of my bed and close my eyes. I would pray, "Please, Jesus, heal my face. When I wake up tomorrow, please give me a whole face with no crooked smile." I would beg God, "Please take away my crooked face so kids don't pick on me anymore." Then I'd go to bed hoping that a miracle would happen while I slept. But every morning I would wake up and anxiously look in the mirror. My face was still crooked.

Then I would go to religion class and hear all about Jesus healing people in the New Testament. If only I had the faith of a mustard seed, I would be healed too. Instead, I felt discouraged, a complete failure, because despite all my prayers and good intentions, nothing ever changed with my face. I still had my crooked smile. I always blamed myself. I must not have had enough faith. Otherwise, surely God would have healed me.

Soon I became an angry little boy with hatred towards others, and I began to lash out. My mother noticed that I was getting into fights at school, so she was the one who taught me how to fight. She got out a boxing book, complete with diagrams, and would demonstrate what I needed to do to defend myself, always preaching to me never to start a fight, but to always finish a fight. She would set up in the kitchen with her one fist up by her face, holding the book in the other hand, explaining how I needed to put my fists up by my face, bend my knees, and stand sideways to my opponent, becoming less of a target.

Unbeknownst to me until years later, my mom used to drive her car every once in a while to the 7-Eleven® across the street from St. Anthony, the Catholic elementary school I attended until the fourth grade. She knew when my playground time would be and she would watch me and pray to God that I would find a friend. Usually what she instead saw were kids standing in groups taunting me, poking fun at me. As I began fighting more and more, kids found out that Nubby could fight and I wasn't the pushover they thought I would be.

The Catholic school nuns used to call my mom to report, "I'm calling because Tommy got in another fight today." They would say, "You know, Mrs. Reis, Jesus would have turned the other cheek." My mom's reply was, "Well, you know, Sister, Jesus was the son of God and, as I recall, he never had a disability nor did he have kids taunting him for it either. So, Sister, I didn't teach Tommy to turn the other cheek. What I taught him is to never start a fight, but always finish a fight." Soon the nuns quit calling her. From then on, whenever I got in a fight, they would turn the other way.

As I approached second, third, and fourth grade, I learned to protect my mom and not tell her the whole truth. Each time I came home, she would quiz me about how things went. Upon hearing all the details, she would express herself, frequently ending up in tears.

So I began to suppress what really went on, and my habitual response to her inquiries about my day would be, "Everything is fine, Mom. Nothing to worry about. It's cool." I felt it was better to lie than see my mother suffer.

I remember Dickey Schraeder, one of my classmates in fourth grade. He would taunt me and poke fun at me when he was amongst all his friends. He wasn't nearly so tough when he was by himself. One day we both had to stay after school and help our teacher clean up as punishment for some now unremembered transgression. Afterwards, *Dickey* had about a 10-minute head start for home as I stayed back to receive a further lecture from my teacher, Mrs. Ban, for my witty, sarcastic mouth, which frequently got me into trouble with teachers and other authority figures.

As soon as I left the school, I planned to track down Dickey and even things up between us. I started running to catch up with him, and as soon as I caught up with him, he started running away from me. After a while, I tackled him and pinned him down, and started pummeling his face with all my pent up anger at what he had done to me all those months before. Soon, I was startled to be picked up by his mom in her efforts to get me off her son. (We must have been right by his house at that point.) Soon, he started punching me back in my face and my gut as his mother held my arms behind my back while she threatened to report all of this to the school.

Another time, Billy Cook, another older neighborhood kid my brother's age (my brother is 4½ years older than me) found me on the way home from school, pinned me down, spit at me, called me all kinds of names, taunted me as he sat on my chest, and hit me, all because I was different. After that incident, word spread one day that Billy Cook was going to come after me after school and hunt me down with a bow and arrow. My sisters got wind of it and surrounded me, escorting me home to protect me from him. Later, my brother confronted Billy Cook and beat him up.

This was the beginning of the bond that was forged between my brother and me. He became my hero, my guardian angel, and my personal protector. My parents always told him to look out for me and protect his younger brother. From then on, if older kids started picking on me on the bus, at the playground, or at school, they had to fight my brother. The amazing thing was, he never lost a fight. Soon he would be fighting kids two or three grade levels ahead of him, and it didn't matter. He never lost. Gangs of kids started going after my brother in retaliation for one of their own getting beat up by him, but they could never catch him. Years later, he qualified for the state track meet in high school, probably from being fleet of foot all those years.

In the Chicago winters, our neighborhood park would flood, allowing kids to figure skate or play hockey. One time, a gang of 20 kids formed a circle from all corners of the rink, in an effort to trap my brother and beat him up, but he somehow found a way to elude them and skate on by.

Of course, Billy Cook and his gang of friends didn't take kindly to my brother beating him up. Soon our own version of a gang war (a bunch of 8- to 12-year-olds) developed between Billy Cook's group and me and my brother's group that included both of my sisters. We called ourselves the Rat Patrol, after a current World War II TV series. We would load our Stingray bikes' baskets with old wrapped up newspapers from my brother's paper route, and fresh, plump tomatoes from my mom's garden, and then swoop down on Billy Cook's group in a hit and run, pummeling them with tomatoes and newspapers. This soon escalated. When I was playing in the park by myself, Billy Cook's group collapsed a small wall of bricks on me, cutting my head open and causing me to go to the hospital. Shortly after I got back, we graduated from tomatoes to rocks. Soon, we were in an all-out rock war that lasted a couple of months, until one time we hit a girl in the eye, causing her to go to a hospital. After that, a truce ensued between us and we didn't hear much from Billy Cook any more.

During this time, my brother was a great baseball player. He was a pitcher who threw a mean fastball and could strike out the side. He could also hit. Each year, he would make the all-star team. Naturally, I got excited about baseball, too, as I watched my brother Bob flourish.

The challenge was, how could I play ball with Nubby? After hours of work among my dad, my brother, and I, we figured out how Nubby could play. I would put the mitt on my left hand—Nubby—and put all my fingers except the thumb on Nubby's hand in the large loop found inside the glove in the area of the small finger. Then I would put my right hand on the outside of the glove. Soon I perfected a way to catch a baseball using both hands.

My brother would throw for hours, and slowly I got better, and started catching more and more balls consistently. He always threw hard to me, because he was a pitcher and he was 4 years older than me. Our family creed was "Tom can do anything anyone else can do." So it never occurred to Bob to cut me any slack. Once when we were on vacation, he grew incredibly frustrated with me because I was dropping everything and letting balls get past me. He got to a point of exasperation, and said, "Look, this sucks. You keep dropping everything. I'm going to wind up and throw at you as hard as I can. If you catch it, I'll stay and keep throwing to you. If you miss, then we're done."

I was petrified!! I was frustrated because he was right. I *was* dropping everything! But he had never wound up before and thrown at me as if he were pitching. I was scared, because I was afraid the ball would hit me and I wouldn't catch it. Next thing I knew, he wound up slowly. My hands were trembling, my heart beating through my chest. I was concentrating with everything I had. Sweat came pouring down my cheeks, and he let it go. The ball was coming so fast, faster than I had ever seen before. I put my mitt out—I'm sure more to protect myself than actually catch the ball. Meanwhile, my brother was convinced that I wouldn't catch it, so as soon as he let it fly, he turned his back to walk away, confident that I wouldn't catch it. *Slap*, the ball came into my mitt, loudly smacking the leather. At the last second, I closed my eyes. As soon as it nestled in my mitt, I closed the other part of the glove with my right hand. I was overcome with glee and surprise as I jumped up and down and shouted to my brother, "I caught it! I caught it!" I don't think I ever saw a more surprised look in my brother's face than when he looked around and saw me holding the ball, with my crooked smile jumping for joy; "I got it. I got it!" We played catch for another couple hours after that.

I soon perfected hitting as well. I would put the knob of the bat in the middle of Nubby's palm and with my right hand grab just above it. I was ready to give baseball a go.

In the Waycinden League of Des Plaines, Illinois, when baseball season came around, we went to a local area school's gymnasium, and everyone would have to try out. Coaches would hit balls to you, watch you throw, and see you hit, and then they would rate you and take turns drafting you for their teams. I was nervous, but I enjoyed these tryouts and meeting my teammates. I could see the doubts on my coaches' faces and my teammate's expressions. If there were cartoon balloons that would pop up about then, they would read, "Why is this kid here? He can't hit. Look at his hand, how is he going to catch anything?"

When I later moved to Burnsville, Minnesota, the team composition was determined by the area of the city you lived in. In Minnesota, my team always sucked, which was frustrating to me because all of my buddies who lived across the street from me, which was the league boundary cutoff, were always on championship teams, while my teams always languished at or near last place.

Nothing brought me greater satisfaction than to see my teammates' skepticism grow into wonder as they could see that I *could* hit, I *could* throw, and I *could* bat. Like my brother before, I became an all-star baseball player my first few years of Little League in Des Plaines and in Burnsville. It was always so cool to prove the doubters wrong.

My confidence and success in baseball allowed me to try other sports—football, tennis, golf, hockey, basketball. I always looked for a way to accommodate Nubby and make it work. If it wasn't for my success in baseball, I'm not sure I would have tried some of the other sports.

I could always easily hide Nubby in my pocket, or prove myself on the athletic field. But with my crooked face, there was nothing I could prove, and there was nowhere to hide. I thought I could hide my face. As an adolescent, I would purposely not smile, in the hopes that no one would see how profoundly crooked it was. To this day, as an adult, I have to remind myself to smile in pictures. The only one I ever fooled was myself.

Babies smile and laugh naturally. I was envious of kids who could just smile freely for the camera. Smiling did not come naturally for me. To smile was to reveal my crooked face even more so. I had to think twice whenever I smiled because it was a continual reminder that I was different. To smile made me vulnerable. It would reveal my differences, making me a target among my peers for ridicule and shame.

Other kids liked having their picture taken, but I didn't. The picture froze in time a reminder of my pain. I wanted so desperately to ignore my crooked face, to pretend it wasn't there, to cover it up. But a picture reminded me of my failure to hide it; it reminded me of a pain I couldn't hide. In some strange way I felt that if I didn't see a picture of my crooked face, then it must not exist.

It became a very lonely existence as I entered adolescence. I had no self-esteem at this point. After years of being told I was ugly by the world, years of being taunted, years of being stared at and told I was something less than human, I came to believe it all. Despite my family's positive messages about me, I grew to believe I was ugly and that I wasn't lovable at all. It didn't help that I was one of the youngest kids in my class, and consequently the smallest kid in my class.

As if my hand and face were not enough of a challenge, I also had to continually deal with this chronic disease that has been with me my whole life, asthma. My last asthma attack happened when I was 8 years old, but I will always remember it. The feeling of struggling to breathe, to take three, four, five breaths to get through one sentence, or feeling the panic well up inside of me as I struggled for air, was almost like drowning.

My asthma was so bad that routinely, each year during the month of August, I was banished to living indoors only, under an air conditioner. My asthma was triggered by hay fever, ragweed, molds, and mildew, or sudden changes in humidity and temperature (common summer occurrences in the Midwest). It would kill me to stay inside and watch my siblings and friends through the window playing outside. Instead, I would play in my room for hours with my blocks and soldiers in solitary confinement.

With my asthma, I was told that I would never be able to run very far, perhaps a hundred yards at most. By the time I was 12 years old, I started taking allergy shots each week as a way to combat allergies triggering my asthma. I ended up taking those shots for 5 years. I felt like a pin cushion, but it never really helped. Once again I was different—no one else in my family had asthma or needed weekly allergy shots.

In the fall of seventh grade, we had a cross-country running unit in my physical education class. The course covered three miles. Because of my asthma, after the instructor took attendance, I would sit and watch as all my classmates would go running. I felt like a caged animal not being able to participate. Each day I would watch them run the course. I would sit back and become more and more frustrated and bored. One day, I said to my teacher, "Hey, let me just try and run as far as I can, and when I'm out of breath, I'll stop and walk." To my amazement, the teacher agreed with my plan. I never told my parents any of this because they didn't think I should be running at all.

The next day, I took off with all of my other classmates and began running the course. I felt invigorated to finally do something besides sitting around waiting for class to end. It felt good to be participating with my classmates. I felt free! The first day I went about 300 yards, and then fell to the ground, withering and gasping for air as all of my classmates ran past me. Slowly I got up, and after the initial panic subsided, after assuring myself that, no, I wasn't going into an asthma attack, I started to walk the course. After a while, I started running again, only to keel over after another 300 yards and start gasping for air again.

This went on for the rest of the semester, but with each passing day, I could go a little farther before I would succumb and start gasping for air. By the end of the second week, I could cover 400 yards before collapsing, and by the fourth week, I was covering 600 yards. Finally, during the last day of the semester, I was able to cover the whole three mile course without stopping. When I came in that final time, my teacher and classmates were at the finish line applauding me and cheering me on. Until that day, I had never had such a feeling of personal accomplishment. Years later, when running became an everyday occurrence, I would periodically run into my old gym teacher, and he would always tip his hat and smile at me as we passed each other, running in opposite directions. In my 30s, I would run and finish two Twin Cities Marathons. Not bad for a kid who could only hope to run 100 yards at a time at best!

By the time I entered high school, my friends and I discovered girls. I, along with half the school, had a crush on Connie Page during sophomore year. If she looked at me and said my name, or said "Hi," I would melt and almost pee in my pants. She was a cheerleader, the most popular girl in our class.

My friends were soon caught up in flirting with girls and asking them to go steady. At the time, my siblings were very involved with the opposite sex as well. Both my sisters were popular cheerleaders—one captained hockey cheerleading and one captained wrestling cheerleading. Meanwhile, my brother was All Conference in football and track and part of that year's Homecoming Court. I would hear about all of my siblings' latest crushes or who they were going out with, and then at school I would hear about my friends and who they were going steady with.

I longed to be a part of that world. No one in my family ever asked me if I was interested in anyone. I suspect that on some level they knew that world was never really open to me, not for someone who looked as different as I did. Every dance I would be envious of my friends and their dates as they would get their tuxes and corsages. I would usually spend the evening of prom shooting baskets by myself in the driveway until late into the night—a very lonely existence. I could look through the window but never be invited in. I lived vicariously through my friends, silently wishing I could be a part of that world, too.

During high school, I never once asked a girl for a date. It seemed so far out of the realm of possibility that someone would actually be interested in me, I never even bothered going there. Instead, I ached inside, wondering if anyone would ever find me lovable and worthy to be with. I suppose the good thing that came out of all of this is that I learned how to be a friend with a woman. They knew I was one of the few guys they could be safe with. They assumed that I had no other agenda with them—and for the most part, I didn't. I was just thrilled that they would be comfortable talking to me and give me the time of day.

During my senior year, however, something amazing happened that would change the course of my life.

# From Dream to Reality

*Dear Bro,*

*Well, this is it, graduation is over and another educa-*
*tion begins . . . .*

*Remember to think. Use your head. Don't expect*
*Grace to dance with you if you're not willing to learn*
*the steps. Think discipline, safety, awareness—and let*
*joy find you by surprise. Learn to expect surprises and*
*wonders, but don't let laziness lull you into danger need-*
*lessly. Let the thoughts that will invade your daytime*
*hours flow through your mind like water. Don't grasp or*
*hold on to them or they will stagnate. Be at peace with*
*your own capacity for silent communion with rhythm,*
*wind, space, and time.*

*Send forth before you each day hopeful thoughts in all*
*you anticipate, that your attitude may conquer the fear in*
*others' hearts of the unknown that you represent.*

*Let not your own fears master you. Maintain a*
*healthy respect for your intuition and sense, but do not let*
*fear be your master. Allow others to be generous with you*
*and remember that the adventure they seek that you share*
*with them is payment enough.*

*Though in the morning, the stars' appearance fades*
*to invisibility, they are still there. So too are our thoughts*

*and prayers for you as you wind toward us in your circular*
*rhythm.*
*Much love,*
*Bro* (May, 1981)

[Letter given to me by my brother to open on the first
day of my bike trip across the United States.]

I announced it at breakfast when I was 13 years old. Growing up,
the kitchen in my house on a school morning was an exercise in
utter chaos. My father was usually long gone by the time my brother
and sisters and I would be scrambling for breakfast in our pursuit of
getting out in time to catch the bus to school at the corner. Usually
my sisters would be arguing because one hogged the bathroom longer
than the other in the primping ritual of looking good for school.
My brother would be downing his orange juice while chewing on a
pop tart. I would be finishing off the last of my Cheerios®. My mom
would be getting lunches packed while smoking a cigarette and
drinking the last drops of her morning coffee.

In this whirlpool of activity, I made my pronouncement to the
world, which consisted of my brother and sisters and my mom:
"Someday, I'm going to bicycle across the US!" This was met with
collective indifference, "That's nice," from my brother as he rushed
out the door, and a, "Could you give me the milk, please?" from my
sister, Mary, not even acknowledging what I had just announced. My
sister Lilly's response was, "What did you say?" as she rushed down
the hall. "Damn it, I didn't know there was a stain on this blouse,"
never listening to my reply. My mom was the only one that seemed
to take it in when she stated, "Well, if anyone can do it, I have no
doubt it will be you, Tom. Dream big!!" Nine years later, I did it.
Upon my graduation from college at 22 years old, I bicycled solo
across America from coast to coast.

The bicycle trip across the United States was done to quench an inner urge for adventure and challenge. Maybe this quest for adventure
runs in my gene pool. My grandpa (yes, my grandpa—he married at

52 years old and was 58 when my mother was born) went West on a covered wagon when he was 12 years old, to Seattle, Washington, in the 1870s. I wanted to do something different. Growing up with a disability always challenged me to find a way to participate, to find a way to overcome and flourish on the playing field. I suppose the trip was another way for me to overcome and flourish.

I had no idea what I had signed up for. The inner adventure far outweighed the adventure on my bike. I had never tested my inner resolve, my mental toughness, as I would on this trip. I have learned that the greatest adventure of my life was never the one on my bike. Rather, it was the adventure within. Thoreau once said, "We should be worthier at the end of our journey then at the beginning." I'd like to think that's true in my case both from the perspective of my bicycle trip and the subsequent journey of my life 30 years later.

> *Lost and alone on some forgotten highway, traveled by many, remembered by few. Looking for something that I can believe in, looking for something that I'd like to do with my life.*
> – John Denver, "Sweet Surrender"

In the back of my mind, I had always thought of going on such an adventure, but I only really started planning the trip in earnest the summer before my senior year in college in Minnesota. That summer, I worked as a counselor at Camp Courage, a camp for people with disabilities ranging in age from 6 to 86 years old. The camp was located about an hour west of the Twin Cities.

There were six cabins at the camp, three for men and three for women. There were twelve campers to a cabin with four counselors. The counselors' quarters were located in the middle of each cabin across from the bathroom. We had a drape for our doorway. The level of care we encountered would be anything from minimal care (e.g., for someone missing a limb) to full care (e.g., for someone who was a quadriplegic). I spent my summer living and working with the disabled 24 hours a day, 7 days a week. The only thing that changed every 2 weeks was the age groups. We started the summer with 6- to 10-year-olds, and finished with the 55 and over Baby Boomers.

You dreaded being woken up in the middle of the night with the word "Counselor." That meant someone needed help going to the bathroom. Since I was the lightest sleeper, that usually meant I was the one answering the call. You would always crawl out in your bare feet and tiptoe with a flashlight into the night in the direction of the camper's voice calling for "Counselor, Counselor," hoping no one else could hear you. Usually, if you woke up someone along the way, others would start clamoring for you to help them to the bathroom as well, which could turn a 5-minute call into a half-hour ordeal.

One night, we had a 19-year-old male quadriplegic who needed his stoma bag (a sack in which his urine would collect) checked and emptied every 3 hours. We set an alarm in the counselor quarters to go off every 3 hours, alerting the next counselor in line to check and empty the stoma bag throughout the night. When it was my turn to go out, I stumbled out of bed, still mostly asleep, at 3:00 in the morning. I crawled on my stomach, knees, and elbows, G.I. Joe™ style, inching my way across the cold floor, going stealth, being as quiet as I possibly could, in my bare feet and underwear, with barely one eye open, as I came upon the quadriplegic's bed. I remember thinking, "Is this a dream or is this really happening?" As I put the flashlight to the bag, inches from my face, still wiping fatigue from my eyes, I squinted to assess just how full the bag was. As I touched the bag to get a reading, the bag of urine immediately exploded in my face, creating an uproar, waking up the camper Joe, and all the campers around him, creating a cacophony of chaos as campers awakened and started calling out the dreaded word "COUNSELOR, COUNSELOR," each wanting immediate help with toileting needs. Of course, there is nothing like a bag full of urine exploding in your face to wake you up fully, ensuring that I would NOT be going to sleep any time soon!

When that kind of "accident" happened (I found out later that the counselor who was to check the bag three hours earlier, had missed his shift, causing the bag to be so full on my shift that it exploded from the mere touch of me checking the bag), the procedure to avoid any kind of contamination (quads are very susceptible to illness and infections of any kind) was to bathe the camper right away, change all of his clothing, make his bed up with fresh linens, and reset his new stoma bag. Sleep was a valuable commodity and all too often I got little of it in my summer working at Camp Courage.

During that summer, I spoke openly to others for the first time about my dream of bicycling across the country after I graduated the following year. We were all about the same age, graduating from college the next year, and we all seemed to share a thirst for adventure. It seemed a fertile time to talk about adventure with others, since we were all entering that time between college and the work-a-day world or graduate school. Before that, the bike trip was just a private dream that I shared with no one. During our free moments, I began recruiting other counselors to join me for this great adventure, and there were indeed some takers. By the end of the summer, six different counselors had signed on, shared the dream, and were planning to go with me the following year.

But as the fall turned to winter and winter turned to spring, one by one they had dropped out of the trip for various reasons (e.g., getting married, finances, entering graduate school, etc.), until, by March of the following year, I was the only one still planning on going. As it became apparent that I would be going solo on my bicycle trip, I began having second thoughts about whether I would go or not. This trip represented the great unknown, and I secretly wondered if I was up for the challenge. It's one thing to imagine something, but quite another to face the reality of my dream. To face that dream alone was still something else.

When I would talk about going solo, it seemed to become people's mission to convince me not to go. I would hear horror stories about how I might be mugged, or murdered, or they would remind me of how little I knew about repairing bikes, and what would happen if I broke down in the middle of nowhere, then what? People who knew I was going on the trip would make it their mission to find any obscure mugging or murder that might appear on page 57 of some paper I never heard of and send it to me with a scrawled note saying, "This could happen to you." My Canadian friends, when I lived in Alberta years later, when I told them I was going to the US (they always referred to the United States as the "Excited States"), would caution me to, "Be careful down there, because people get shot down there."

After a while, the negativity would become suffocating and I wanted to yell, "Enough! I'm tired of hearing all the *what ifs*. They are all so negative!" I remembered the quote by Ashleigh Brilliant (can this really be the name of a philosophy professor at the University of California?), "If you are really, really careful, you'll do nothing."

The adventure was there for the taking, and I refused to be derailed by other people's fears. Besides, I surmised, if Creation is good and God is good, then my belief was that, in facing an unknown on this trip, I had a better chance for good happening than something bad happening. A new reason emerged for going on this trip, after hearing all the negativity. I wanted to go on the trip to prove to people that good things can happen, not just bad things, when embracing the unknown.

It wasn't until spring break that March that I sorted things out in my mind and decided that I still would go through with the bike trip, even if it meant that I would be bicycling alone. To further solidify the idea, I bought a brand new Fuji 12-speed bicycle. It was an ugly brown with revolutionary shifters not on the frame of the bike, but located at the end of each handle bar (the latest development in bicycle technology at the time). This was the vehicle of my dreams. With a nervous sigh, I plopped down $500 and bought my bike. It was the ugliest 12-speed I had ever seen, but for almost 3 months, it would be my vehicle of choice across this vast country.

Unfortunately, this brand new bike sat in the living room of my apartment, shiny and new, as I waited for winter to finally ease its chokehold on Duluth and let the thaw of spring arrive. There was no spinning on an indoor bike while waiting for spring, since our recreation center on campus had nothing of the sort. The snow had been particularly deep, and had only thawed enough to go biking around mid-April. I had only a month to get ready for the trip!

I remember how ill prepared I was for this trip. I found my old bicycle log, in which I had tabulated my miles of training each day in '81, and it was embarrassing to look at. For one 1-week stretch it read: "April 6 = 12 miles; April 7 = 14 miles; April 8 = 10 miles." The grand total for mileage for the week was 57 miles, and that was riding with no weight or panniers on the bike! On the first day of my bike trip in Oregon, I had gone 70 miles, more than I had covered in an entire week of training in Duluth! In riding on the trip, the first 10 to 20 miles were just a warm-up to my day.

I graduated from the College of St. Scholastica on Saturday, May 23, 1981—a memorable day, not only because I graduated from college that day, but also because I had been chosen by my class to be the valedictorian and give the graduation speech. It was a particularly cold and dreary day, even for Duluth standards. Duluth is the only place I know of where on the top of the hill you can get an ice cream cone but by the time you get to the shore of Lake Superior it is not unusual to see the temperature drop 20 degrees and you find yourself looking for a hot chocolate in the middle of July. Down by the lake, near the convention center where the ceremony took place, the clouds were very low, like they were dipping in to the lake. It was raining on and off all day, the kind of day that, no matter what you did, you couldn't warm up. In my ideal world, such a day would be best spent sitting close to a fire, snuggled in a blanket, sipping hot chocolate, and reading a book. This wasn't an ideal world. I was getting ready to speak to a couple thousand people.

It was more than ironic that I was chosen to give the graduation address. One of the reasons why I'd chosen St. Scholastica was because it was one of the few colleges that didn't require a speech class. I was deathly afraid of public speaking. Apparently, I'm not alone. I read somewhere in the hierarchy of common fears, public speaking is our number one fear, and death is number two. I had not taken a speech class (Hey, it wasn't a requirement!), and now I'm giving my first speech in front of the graduating class, faculty, staff, and families. To say I was nervous and had some slight trepidation in wondering if I could pull this off was more than an understatement.

Of course I couldn't give a speech that was light and fluffy—about what a great time we had, how the 4 years had flown by—and end it with a famous quote by a long-dead U.S. president, all to be soon forgotten amidst the graduation dinners and parties afterward. And no, I couldn't run my speech by Sister Timothy Kirby, the Director of Student Life at St. Scholastica, who had given me multiple subtle hints that she should look at it for quality control purposes. No, I wanted to surprise everyone. I succeeded. I did surprise everyone. I gave the longest graduation speech ever given at the college! It was so long that, for years afterward, that's what I was known for. Every time I stepped on campus and ran in to the college president, he inevitably brought it up about my longest speech ever. I'm so glad he has long since retired!

I didn't want to give a speech on something meaningless and fluffy. No, I had to give a speech on "Becoming." I wanted to address something of substance, which unintentionally ended up alienating the faculty and my parents as I criticized both along the way. Good thing I was facing the audience and had my back to the faculty. I hate to think what it would have been like to actually look into their faces and read their reactions to some of the things I had said. For instance, one of the things I railed about was how education focused so much on training people for a career, with so little focus on training people to be well-rounded, to become better human beings. I laugh at that statement today, as an educator teaching at the college level for the past 20 years, thinking how much more we were focused on students getting a well-rounded, liberal arts education back then as compared to today's college standards.

I survived my moment of glory in part because of my brother. I had been nervous and preoccupied all day, with my speech heavy on my mind. We had a graduation mass for graduates and their families, throughout which I was especially comatose. At the brunch afterwards, I couldn't eat a thing because I was so nervous. Finally, as the moment arrived and I approached the lectern on the stage to give my speech that afternoon, just as I looked up, my brother and some friends unfurled a huge banner from the top balcony, on black paper with big yellow bold lettering on it, that said, "Fly, don't die!" (My nickname in college was "The Fly," who was the cool main character from the movie *Carwash*.) As soon as I saw the sign, I broke out laughing, which was the perfect antidote to break the tension as I launched into my speech.

Within a few days, I was in Denver, staying with my brother in a seminary dormitory as I was preparing for my flight to Portland, Oregon. After purchasing my plane ticket, I had about $800 to my name, and that's all I had to get me from one coast to the other and then home again. I had no credit cards and there were no cell phones back then. To this day, I wonder how I did it.

The next day, I was getting ready to go to the airport when I couldn't get my bike all taken apart and boxed up. Even my brother looked at me in my struggles and said, "This isn't a good sign. You can't even take apart your bike, and you are going to ride cross-country!" It was so bad that I missed my flight to Portland. Luckily, this took place in the early '80s, when, if you missed a flight, you weren't penalized. When I finally did get to the airport, I just looked at the flight board and picked the next flight to Oregon. Instead of flying to Portland, in a cavalier, naïve way, I said, "Oh what the heck, I've never been to Eugene. Let's just go there."

I remember on the flight as I passed over the Rockies, I kept looking at one snowcapped mountain after another, as far as I could see, and just then it struck me, the magnitude of what I had undertaken. I thought to myself just then, "Holy shit, what did I get myself into?" I felt a deep foreboding[ as a wave of fear washed over me. Suddenly, I felt a surge of terror and dread like I had never felt before. The cold reality hit me. "I'm really doing this. I'm going solo and there is no one to help me, no one to rescue me. I am beyond the point of no return. I can't turn back now." For a moment, I thought, "Maybe this is a dream, and maybe I'll just wake up in the comfort of my bed and the warmth of my room and wait for the alarm to go off and send me on my way." But there was no ringing alarm, and I knew this was no dream. I thought to myself, "Man, I'm going to be biking over these mountains for the days and weeks ahead. From this plane, I can see snow-covered mountains as far as I can see in any direction, and I'm 30,000 feet up in the air!" I lost all appetite for dinner. Instead, I ordered a 7UP® to calm my upset stomach as I quietly wrote in my journal, my new best friend, about the magnitude of what lay ahead of me in the coming weeks and months.

I landed in Eugene, Oregon the night of May 27, 1981, my first time ever flying anywhere by myself. I felt happy to collect all my belongings and find a taxi to take me to a nearby motel and plan my next move. I decided to put this coast-to-coast adventure in perspective. I would bicycle the 70 miles to a town called Florence, Oregon and dip my toes in the Pacific Ocean. I love the ocean and to be this close and not go there would have made no sense. Besides, I meant it when I said I would be biking "coast to coast!"

A beautiful day for a ride, the temperature was in the mid-60s, and it was sunny, with a gentle breeze blowing. I didn't sleep well that night, anticipating embarking on Day 1 of my coast-to-coast adventure. This was the first time I had packed everything in the panniers, and God, I felt loaded down!! It was considerably harder just getting my bike going with all this extra weight. It took some time and adjustment to get used to steering my bike with all the extra weight on my handlebars and front wheels. I was so glad that I had brought some extra bungee cords to lash down the additional supplies that I could not contain in my panniers. I looked like the *The Grapes of Wrath*, only on a bike, with stuff spilling out of my panniers and extra tires and equipment lashed on top of my back fender. It was amazing that I never lost anything. I was happy with the modifications that were made for my bike specifically for this trip. I had had extra padding put on the handlebars to ease the incessant pounding from the road, and I had had my squeeze brakes reversed so that on the left side of my handlebars, I could use Nubby to push down on the brake rather than the much more awkward, standard maneuver of pulling the brake toward me.

Bicycling was considerably harder, in fact harder than I had ever done before because (a) now I was riding through coastal mountains, the likes of which I had never encountered in Minnesota, and (b) it was the first time I had ever bicycled with my panniers filled with supplies. The going was much more difficult heading into a wind coming from the west, and continually riding up and down hills with a fully loaded bike. The weight, not only over my back tire but over my front tire as well, made steering the bike even more of a challenge.

That day I rode my bike further than I had ever ridden before, 70 miles. I bicycled more in one day, fully loaded than I had for entire weeks in my "training" for the trip. I also encountered my first of nine flats on the trip. I didn't do well with that, either. It happened on a busy two-lane stretch of highway about 2 p.m., 20 miles from the sea. It took me almost an hour to change the flat. My tools were tucked away in one of the panniers and I had the hardest time identifying where the puncture was on the tire. By the time I had fixed the flat and figured out how to get the tire properly mounted and secured on my frame, it looked like a disaster area, as half of my supplies were strewn all over the shoulder of the road. My hands were black and full of grease, and I had so much stuff piled on top of my panniers that I looked more like a refugee escaping a war-torn country than someone on a bike trip. The important thing was that I had faced my first bike repair and, though I was anything but smooth or efficient, I figured it out successfully, and got up on my bike and back on the road.

The highlight of the day was seeing the seagulls flying above me, still 20 miles from the beach, giving me a hint that the ocean was near. Then, within a couple of miles, I could smell the fresh, salty, sea air, which stirred my anticipation of seeing the ocean and pulled me forward. Growing up in the Midwest and seeing the ocean only one other time in my life, my flagging, tired spirit became rejuvenated when, about a mile away, I could begin to hear the faint sound of the ocean surf crashing on to the shore. When I did finally see the ocean, I was filled with awe at its immensity. It was a perfect day to be at the beach. The sun was shining, it was warm, and the sky was blue. I couldn't wait to pitch my tent and walk on the beach, feeling the cold sand between my toes, as the cold ocean water rushed up to surround my feet, quickly rising to my calves only to recede back as quickly as it had come. That night, I experienced something I had never done before. I fell asleep serenaded by the melodic, back-and-forth flow of waves crashing on the beach and then receding back to their place of origin, the sea. Now all I had to do was point my bike east and peddle over 3,000 miles into the unknown until I reached the other shore—easier imagined or said to myself than actually done, of course.

There is a picture of me next to my bike, fully loaded, with the Pacific Ocean in the background. I look at that picture today and I am struck by how young I looked and how naïve I was. I had no idea what I was in for. I'm reminded of a quote I grew up with: "Life isn't fair. It gives you the tests first and the answers afterwards." There were plenty of tests ahead of me, and I would have to live into the answers.

Oregon was my training state. It is unfortunate that the most beautiful state I bicycled in was also the most painful. After the first day, and for the rest of the state, I was most comfortable on my bike. As soon as I would get off my bike to walk around, I would waddle like a penguin, I was in so much pain and discomfort. My calves, knees, and thighs felt incredibly stiff, and each step was made with intention and pain. It felt like I was on a trail of tears. I moved about as fast as an old man on a walker.

When I purchased my bike, I got a Brooks saddle for my seat. This was considered the best saddle made. I didn't get why it was so good. It seemed pretty hard and stiff to me, but what did I know? I knew nothing about bicycles and saddles, so I bought it.

Once on the trip, that saddle seemed to get harder with every passing day. My biking day consisted of continually switching from one butt cheek to the other on my Brooks saddle, in my constant search for comfort. As soon as one cheek started feeling numb and sore, I would switch over to the other cheek. I did this routine throughout the entire 3,000 miles of my trip, and I was never comfortable.

When I would periodically stop at bike shops, inevitably the staff would nod with approval when they would see my Brooks saddle. I didn't have much padding on my bum to begin with, but the pounding on my saddle was killing me. There was no way I could think of biking across the United States on this saddle. I became a constant source of complaints throughout the trip. The standard refrain I would get to my complaining in bike shops would be "Oh, just give it time. You've just got to give it time to break in."

The only thing that seemed to break in on the entire trip was my butt!!! I gave that saddle over 3,000 miles to break in, and it never did. On my Canadian trip, 28 years later, I made sure my butt would be going in comfort. I not only had gel filled biking shorts (I hadn't known such a thing existed) but padded biking underwear. In fact, I would wear two pairs of padded underwear underneath my padded biking shorts on a nicely padded seat. I also bathed my vital parts and rear end in Chamois biking butter/lubricant to prevent chaffing and open sores before departing each day. The amazing thing is that, with all that padding, I still ended up developing a saddle sore. I get sore even today just thinking about all the time I spent riding in that Brooks saddle in the hopes that, one day, it would break in. I'm sure that saddle is in some dump somewhere, and I bet, after all these years, it still isn't broken in!

I brought three books on my trip; a journal, *Walden* by Henry David Thoreau, and Cervantes' *Don Quixote*. In fact, I nicknamed my bicycle after Don Quixote's horse, Rocinante. I brought the books with me because they were classics in literature and I thought on some level they would speak to me within the adventure I was having. Besides, I knew I would be spending lots of time alone and I love to read.

In Oregon, I discovered the beauty of the Three Sisters Wilderness area and Bend, Oregon. While biking in this area, I ran in to my first bicyclist on the trip. One night while I was camping, I shared a campsite with Bill.

Bill was in his early 50s and he, too, was biking by himself. He was a lawyer from Boston. He was a skinny man with short black hair parted neatly to the side. After 3 days on the road, I welcomed the opportunity to share a campsite with a fellow traveler, not to mention another bicycle adventurer. Traveling solo, Bill looked like he welcomed company too, so that night, we struck up a conversation around the campfire.

I'm not sure what it is about me, but once you get past my differences, my disabilities, people find me easy to engage. My Mom told me when I was growing up that people are most interested in and comfortable talking about themselves. It is a lesson I have always remembered and so, in meeting new people, I have always been curious and asked lots of questions. The occasional person may have found my questioning too invasive, but most people welcome the opportunity to break the ice and talk about themselves. Bill was one who liked to talk about himself, which fit well with my natural curiosity and propensity for asking questions.

Later that night, in the quiet of my tent under my flashlight, I journaled about the day's events, a ritual I followed before turning in every night on the road. I would write pages at a time, in which I could pour out all the thoughts of my day. Never since have I had so much time alone, pouring out my thoughts out on written pages as I did on this trip. I was amazed at how much Bill shared with me at the fire, particularly about his current marital situation. He was separated due to an affair he was having. He also talked about losing his son to a car accident and how devastated he was after that. At first, it surprised me how much he shared, but then, as I reflected further, it didn't surprise me at all. After all, he would never see me again. Perhaps I was his pseudo-confessional. He shared with me things I would imagine he wouldn't be sharing with too many other people, including his estranged wife. Apparently this trip by himself was his opportunity to find himself. I hoped, for his sake, that he succeeded. Little did I realize that his affair and the loss of his son would be something I would visit years later in my own marriage.

By the time I reached eastern Oregon and pulled into the town of Ontario on the Idaho border, I had been on the road about a week. I was beginning to be able to walk around without constant pain with each step I took. I was starting to walk much more like a human being, no longer resembling a penguin.

CHAPTER 4

# My Greatest Loss

Little did I realize that the things Bill shared with me at the campsite in rural central Oregon would all come to pass in my own life, 16 years later, in a place far from my imagination in that summer of 1981.

I noticed her smile first, and the fact that she was wearing a summer dress when no one else was wearing a dress, and it looked so good on her. As my friends and I use to say when checking out pretty women, "She curved where she was supposed to curve." It was August 1985, and move-in day at the residence hall for graduate students. I was attending graduate school, earning a master's degree in Human Development and Family Studies at Kansas State University, which means I was studying to become a marriage and family therapist. I had been on campus a week earlier getting a head start on work for my assistantship.

The graduate hall was home to students from over 75 countries. It was so international that I thought it would be appropriate to have the UN flag waving out front. Just what a kid from Minnesota was doing in the international hall was beyond me, but it would be my home for the next 2 years. Mona was moving in from her home, Canada, and would be living just down the hall from me.

My marriage and family therapy program was a very small program in a campus of close to 19,000 students. We had around a dozen students in total. I was pleasantly surprised when I discovered that Mona was in my program as well. By the following January we were dating, and for the next 2 years, we lived in the same hall, attended many of the same classes, and shared many of the same cases as co-therapists. By the time she graduated in September of 1988, we were married. We were what I use to call "the two look couple." People would take a second look at her because of her beauty and they would take a second look at me because of my disabilities. I suppose at the time I was enthralled that someone so pretty could find me attractive on some level too—not something that had happened very much in my life as a person with a disability up to that point.

We were married for almost 9 years. The first 3 years we lived in Minnesota. Mona was very homesick for Canada, homesick specifically for her native Alberta. I knew she desperately wanted to go back, and being a person always open for adventure, I agreed that if she found a job in Alberta, we would relocate there. My mother grew up in Washington State. She had a firm sense of home and hated the Midwest where she raised her children. In the first 14 years of marriage, she went home twice, once to bury her father and once to bury her mother. I remembered my mother's deep sorrow and her longing to go back home to Washington. I didn't want that to happen to Mona. So by the end of 1991, we had indeed moved to Prince Thomas, Alberta. I use to say to my friends, "Just go north to the Klondike and turn left and that's where you will find me." Prince Thomas wasn't quite the Arctic Circle, but it was over 500 miles north of Edmonton. Prince Thomas was in the middle of the province, about 300 miles from the coast, a city of 60,000 or so people, known as the Capitol of the North. You knew you were up north when "Deer Crossing" signs were replaced by "Moose Crossing" signs. I lived there for close to 9 years. In Prince Thomas, I lived through my greatest sorrow.

Graduate school provided an illusion of commonality for Mona and me; living in the same hall, studying together, going to the same classes, and sharing cases was our world, and we spent most of our time in that world together. But once we both graduated from school and got settled in the "real world," we discovered we had very little in common.

I knew the marriage was a mistake by 6 or 7 months in to it. I had kept a journal since my senior year of high school, but I never read it while I was married. I thought it would be too depressing to revisit. (After my divorce, I did reread all of the journals that I wrote while I was married and I was right; they were depressing to read!)

To paraphrase Thoreau's *Walden*, it was a time of quiet desperation for me. I lived a life in a small piece of hell. I couldn't tell anyone of my loneliness, frustration, or pain. After all, certainly two well-trained marriage and family therapists should be able to work out any difficulties that might arise, or so I thought. No one else in the family could know that we, of all people—the so-called *experts*—could be struggling to make our marriage work. On the surface everything looked fine. Our personalities complimented each other well, and we were both established professionals in the community. But within the four walls of our home, and much to my horror, I had recreated my parents' marriage; we lived separate and apart lives. We shared a house and that was about all we shared. We operated more as roommates than husband and wife.

My parents lived in a "match made in hell." They had spent nearly 60 years of their lives married but were miserable living together. They were in a relationship called in research an "empty shell marriage," a marriage in which the couple stays together for a variety of reasons like money, security, or predictability, but one in which the love they once knew that had brought them together has long since died.

They stayed together for years because they were devout Catholics who didn't believe in divorce. They had resided in separate bedrooms for years, in part because after my birth and near death, it was discovered that they had an Rh factor that would make any further pregnancies very difficult. The doctor told them that another pregnancy would likely kill my mother. Separate bedrooms were the solution, as birth control was not on option for a devout Catholic couple. In living with Mona, I could see more and more familiarity with my own parents' pathetic relationship. It scared the shit out of me.

I knew that marriage was tough work. I call marriage the "semi-nary of the soul," and ours was no exception. But I took my vows seriously (no one until then had ever divorced in my family) and I (the marital/family therapist) was determined to make it work. I found myself envious of my friends' marriages. Usually, the first year or two tended to be the most difficult, but with each subsequent year, as their love and intimacy grew, their marriages seemed to get better and better. But for me, it felt like I was constantly rolling a big, heavy rock up a steep hill, only to slip and fall near the top and have it roll all the way down; I would have to pick myself up and start all over again rolling that rock up the hill. Unlike my friends' marriages, I noticed that with each passing year, it wasn't getting any easier. In fact, there seemed to be less and less for us to talk about. I could feel us becoming strangers.

When I would go on annual whitewater canoe trips with my buddies, they would make their obligatory calls home each evening to their wives. They couldn't wait to check in with their wives and regale them with the stories of the day. They would have so much to talk about and there would be so much laughter in their conversations. Meanwhile, I would be straining if I could talk for more than 10 minutes with Mona; there was just so little that I wanted to share (or that she was interested in hearing.)

In my experience both as a therapist and an educator, what we know is that marriages usually don't end in any kind of explosion; marriages end in a whimper. Two people grow apart and eventually they get lonely and disillusioned. The relationship becomes no longer a priority, and the marriage fades away. One day you wake up and you no longer recognize the person to whom you made a vow.

Meanwhile, Mona's biological clock was ticking. I was commit-ted to the relationship; there was no way I was going to leave. Even though I was unhappy in the relationship, I still liked the idea of becoming a father. So we started the process of trying to become pregnant.

I had a sense of entitlement with pregnancy. I thought that once you decided to become pregnant, it would be like walking down the next aisle in the local grocery store, picking something off the shelf, and, the next thing you know, you're pregnant, no big deal.

But we soon discovered that it was a big deal. Try as we did, we were not getting pregnant. Soon we did fertility tests on both of us and, much to my horror, I was the problem. Apparently, my sperm lacked motility and there was an overly high percentage of sperm that were abnormal.

I hated being defective. My whole life I had been the defective one. Just once, I thought to myself, couldn't it be that I was not the problem!?! Early on, I remember, when we were both being tested to see where the fertility problem was, having a conversation with Mona about it. I said, "You know, Mona, if it ends up that you are the problem, we'll get through this. I will still love and support you through this. I'm confident we will find another way to resolve this."

It was haunting when I asked her what would happen if I was the problem. She said, "I'd be pissed! I'd be really disappointed." There was no reassurance of support or love for me, no optimism of "We'll get through this." None of that. I prayed to God in that moment, "Please God, just once, let me not be the problem!"

When the fertility testing results showed that I was indeed the problem, Mona was devastated. I tried to comfort her, to no avail. How could I, the source, the cause of her great disappointment, be her main source of comfort as well? I was the one to blame and I felt it. There was no cushioning the blow. She was pissed and disappointed and she let me know it. Infertility is a silent, private grief. She became even more distant from me. People had no clue about our infertility problems, so in social situations, when they would tease us about "Why don't you have kids yet?" they had no idea how much those comments cut to the core and how hurtful they felt.

I started going to a naturopath in the hopes that he could solve our fertility problems. Each month he would test my sperm after treatments and indeed my sperm count was improving. So when we became pregnant 6 months later, it did not seem out of the realm of possibility. We had sex so rarely that when we found out Mona was pregnant in late April, it made sense. I had no suspicion that she was impregnated by someone else. Then in June, with our first ultrasound, we discovered we were pregnant with twins. My mom informed me that twins ran on her side of the family with some distant cousins, so it all made sense to me.

When we finally announced we were pregnant, our friends, families, and colleagues came up to us and congratulated us. I wanted none of it. I played the part of being excited and saying all the right things, but inside I felt so trapped and scared, because I knew our marriage was on shaky ground. I felt backed in to a corner. Now there was no way out. But this woman I felt miserable with was now going to be the mother of my children. I was determined to make this relationship work once and for all. Yet as the months advanced into the pregnancy and Mona grew bigger and bigger, my efforts to be a better husband and partner, were met with continual setbacks and failure. I grew more disenchanted and resigned myself to a life of emptiness and despair. The emptiness I felt was like a giant cavern in my heart.

After the boys were born, we only made it 9 more months before I asked to separate. Mona's mom had been going through her own separation from Mona's dad and so, conveniently, she lived with us before the boys were born and after they had arrived. She was a lifesaver. Her expertise as a retired nurse and mother of three babies was an immense help. Things would have been a lot tougher if Mary Ellen hadn't been there to help us and serve as a buffer between Mona and me.

Whenever Mary Ellen was gone, Mona and I would fight. Each month it seemed to get progressively worse. In the end, I decided to separate because I didn't want our marriage to be the primary relationship model for our boys. You hear of people "staying together for the kids." In our case, I wanted to separate because of the kids. We had become my parents' empty marriage and I wanted no part of that. So on September 13, 1997 I moved out, and Mona and I worked through the courts for joint custody and joint guardianship.

When I moved out, I was seen by the greater community as the bad guy. How could Tom move out on Mona when she has two little babies? The dean of the college where I was a professor found me one day in the library. Rachael was the godmother of our oldest son.

She took me aside and basically told me that my moving out was a mistake. "Mona is the best thing you've got going for you."

In the spring of 1998, friends began to tell me that neither of the boys looked like me. By that time, they were close to 6 months old and began showing more distinct characteristics of their own unique features.

For quite some time, I had been suspicious of Mona having an affair with her coworker and fellow therapist, Nick. The year before, during Valentine's Day we were housesitting our neighbor's home while they were on vacation. They happened to have a large hot tub that we visited periodically while they were gone. On Valentine's night, Mona and I were in the hot tub along with Nick. I retired around 10 p.m. because of teaching an early class the next morning. I left thinking Mona would not be far behind. I was awakened at 2 a.m. as she finally made it back to bed. I remember it well because it was one of the rare times that she was actually interested in initiating sex with me. I did question her later but she denied any wrongdoing and made up some excuse that must have seen plausible at the time since I didn't give it any more serious thought.

When you love someone and are committed to the relationship, signs of infidelity can be quite blatant, but because I was not looking for that, I completely missed them until much later, in piecing things back together in hindsight. For instance, I should have been highly suspicious when I found out later that during a company retreat in lower Alberta, Mona and Nick spent 2 extra days touring hot springs together before coming back to Prince Thomas. Or the time the company would pay for them to have dinner together every Tuesday night after they were out of town together providing therapy at satellite centers in outlying communities. I went to one of these dinners where they were supposed to "debrief" and I felt like a fifth wheel with my own wife. Their dinner felt more and more like date night than any debriefing session. Very little of their dinner was devoted to their work and the clients they had seen that day.

After I moved out, Nick started showing up more and more at Mona's house. The neighbor with whom I shared hockey season tickets would tell me how each evening he would walk around the neighborhood before retiring for the night with his little 3-year-old girl, and he would see Nick's car parked all around the neighborhood. Then when he got up in the morning and looked out the dining room window, he reported that it was not unusual to see Nick exit Mona's home through the sliding glass door and hop the backyard fence on his way home. Shortly after I had moved out, Nick had separated from his wife. She subsequently packed up and left Prince Thomas to move back home to Ontario, taking their 10-year-old daughter with her.

That spring, I came down with an initial bout of kidney stones and after hospitalization, I asked my urologist, who had done the initial testing of my sperm, the odds of me fathering children, given my profile. He told me that, given my profile, I had about a 1 in 10,000 chance of ever fathering children. When I asked him about my suspicions about actually fathering my children and the possibility of paternity testing, he encouraged me to, "Let sleeping dogs lie. You've got your children, Tom. You're a father now, something you always wanted to be. Don't upset the apple cart."

But it began to gnaw at me more and more. What happens if I'm not really the father of my boys? I asked Mona directly about it one day as she stopped by my townhome to pick up the boys. I told her, "I'm thinking of getting a paternity test to see if the boys are really my boys." I explained what the urologist told me about the situation. Then I said, "But you know the truth, Mona. Why don't you spare me the $1,000 it will cost me to get the test? Why don't you tell me now if the boys are mine?"

She replied, "Suit yourself, Tom. Go get the test and see for yourself," as she walked out of my home with the boys in tow.

That summer, I decided to work as a volunteer in the Glacier Peak Wilderness area of the North Cascade Mountains in the state of Washington. At my college, there was no summer school, and I saw this as an opportunity to get away on a cheap "working vacation." While I was there, I received a typewritten letter from Mona, after I had gone on a 12-hour hike that day. It was the last thing I expected to receive.

In the letter, Mona told me for the first time that Kelly and Ryan were not my sons. She told me about the 3-plus years that she and Nick had been having the affair. I was devastated by the news. I was in a wilderness setting 40 miles from any roads. There was no cell coverage or computers or phones. I felt so isolated and devastated in my grief. I had no family or friends to reach out to in my moment of grief. Though I had my suspicions, I thought there was a 90% chance that the boys were still my biological children.

Later, on what would have been our 10th anniversary, the paternity testing confirmed what Mona had told me in the letter. Here is what I wrote on that fateful day in my journal:

*September 3, 1998*

> *Today I found out officially, on what would have been our 10th anniversary (How ironic!!!), that Kelly and Ryan are not my biological children. I knew pretty much that they were not after what Mona had told me in the letter back in June. Still, it's quite shocking when you get the cold, hard data. I didn't even get the dignity of a letter. There was no, "Dear Tom." They just sent me this computer printout that says, "Probability of biological fatherhood is 0.00%."*
>
> *This felt like a terminal illness in which you expect someone to die, but once you've heard they died, it still shocks you. It catches you in mid-breath, and you don't know whether to exhale further or inhale.*
>
> *I was devastated with the news. This was not the result I was banking on. My heart was beating madly as I tried to come to grips with this latest revelation. My mind raced to various scenarios: Would I never see them again? Who is the real father and would he re-enter the boys' lives? Or would I then be treated as an "uncle"? None of these scenarios appealed to me at all. The one thing I knew was that they were my boys (regardless of what the test said) and I loved them dearly. Yet I sensed that with*

*this news, things would never be the same again. I never knew the truth could be so devastating.*

*So in a metaphorical sense, it felt like my kids died that day. The difference was that in my case, there would be no obituary or eulogy, no memorial service, funeral, or gravestone to mark the event. All that is left to bear witness to this occasion is my broken heart.*

*After I got the news in the mail that day, I walked up to the boys' room. The cribs seemed so empty and still. The toys were scattered about the room, lifeless, like corpses. They made no sound.*

*No one knew the pain and anguish that I felt. I felt like a little boy who wants to cry out in church, but whose mouth is muzzled by his mother's hand at the very moment he wants to scream out with all his might.*

*I went for a long walk that evening after I received the news. I noticed the wind felt a bit colder that day than usual. It hinted that winter was close by. It felt like winter had already arrived in my heart. This is such a private grief. It's like someone who has been sexually abused; they look the same as you or me. No one knows from the outside the private horror they've experienced.*

*I kept hearing the line from Canadian artist Bruce Cockburn's songs ringing in my ears: "Joy will find a way. Joy will find a way. Come quickly, my joy, and rescue me. Come take me from this place of despair."*

Thus began the most difficult period of my life, my dark night of the soul.

By this time, Nick had moved in with Mona and the boys. I still desired to be in the boys' lives, like perhaps as a stepfather or something. We met at a therapist's office to discuss what the future would look like now that Nick wanted to be in the picture.

It is one thing to know about an affair, but it was hard to stomach seeing my not-yet-ex-wife holding Nick's hand as they came in together for the session with the therapist. The rest of the story came out in the session. Nick impregnating Mona was his "gift" to her. The plan was for him to impregnate her and walk away with me never knowing about their little secret. I couldn't believe what I was hearing. I saw the divorce coming and even the affair, but the whole idea of impregnating my wife and keeping this as a secret sounded like a made-for-TV movie. I couldn't believe that this was part of the script of my life.

It became clear that they did not see me in any type of father role with the boys. They wanted me to become less as Nick became more in their lives. After 21 months, they were telling me, Nick would take it from here, as if I was passing a baton to him in a race, no big deal! But it was a big deal to me. I named the boys. I wrote their baptismal ceremony. I stayed up with them many a night caring for them. Except for the biology, they were my boys and would always be my boys.

It was clear that I would be going to the courts after that meeting to fight to be in my boys' lives. Mona didn't want me to have any part in their lives because "it would be too confusing having two father figures in their lives." That didn't make any sense to me since in today's families there are numerous instances where children have both a biological father and a stepfather. I thought I could at least be a stepfather, but Mona and Nick wanted no part of that.

By January of 1999, I had already spent thousands of dollars in legal fees fighting to be in the boys' lives, in what would be a lost cause. I stood before the judge as he announced his verdict: Mona would get full custody, full guardianship over the boys. Biology is destiny; because I had no genetic link to the boys, I had no legal rights to be in the boys' lives. I had lost. If I was to ever see the boys again, it would only be through Mona's consent.

As I was leaving the courtroom, I had run into Mona, as she was late for the hearing. She asked what happened, and I told her, "You won, Mona. You get everything," and then I walked away. I wrote the following in my journal for that fateful day:

*January 13, 1999*

*God, I never thought this day would come! In a matter of 5 minutes standing in front of a judge, my life has changed forever. Mona has it all now: full custody, full guardianship, and full control over access.*

*I walked out of court that day without my coat on, in my suit and tie. It was grey, overcast, and cold outside, but I didn't care. All the color in the world felt lost to me in my depression. Sometimes I think it is easier to die than to live. I put one foot in front of the other as if I were aging with each step, feeling dazed and battered, slowly making my way down the street to my van, oblivious to the cold. I got in to my van and I felt like driving forever into the distance. Anyplace has got to be better than here!*

*Then I thought of the boys and drove over to the day care and played with them. They had no clue of what I was feeling or how big a day this was. They didn't need to be concerned with all this adult stuff. I just had to see and touch and hold the boys close, on this day in particular. I just wanted to hug them and hold them close, watch them smile and giggle. It's good they will never know any of this. I wouldn't want them or anyone to feel this pain.*

*Later that night at home, I walked around the house in silence. I went to the bathroom and saw their bathtub toys ringing the tub. I saw the little bottle of baby shampoo next to my shampoo. I wondered if I would ever be able to give them a bath again.*

*I opened the doors to their rooms. I saw the covers all messed up like they had just left the scene, their teddy bears standing guard as if waiting for the boys' next visit. The room felt chilly and dark, like the space in my heart. If I listen hard enough in the darkness, it's like I can almost hear their little voices filled with laughter.*

*How I wish they had left some kind of scent on their covers so I could breathe them in and bring them back to life in this barren place.*

*So this is what grief is like—this pining, this knot in my stomach, this constant swallowing and anxiousness. The flip side of the coin of love is always grief. How I wish things were different!*

It would be almost 4 months before I would see the boys again. It was on Easter Sunday. I missed them so much and I knew they would be at church. I made sure before I walked in that I saw their car in the parking lot. I came in late and stood in the back. There they were in front of me, near the front of the church, with their backs turned towards me, kneeling with their mom, dad, and grandma. I wrote further about this moment in my journal:

*April 4, 1999 (Easter)*

*Then at communion, an extraordinary thing happened. Ryan went up to communion with Gramma holding his hand. When you turned down the aisle, Ryan, you saw me! You kept walking toward me past your pew, bringing Gramma and Kelly with you. I looked at Gramma and saw tears coming down her cheeks. Then I looked down at the boys and they had their arms outstretched to me, looking up wanting me to pick them up.*

*I reached down to pick them up at the back of the church and was greeted with laughter and wet kisses, the kind only 2-year-olds can give. I was hugging them and holding them, while communion was going on, telling them how much I loved them, I glanced up and saw Mona and Nick quickly gathering up their things and walking toward us. I held them close to my heart, squeezing them tighter, knowing these were stolen moments, like moments when a loved one slips momentarily out*

47

*of a coma. Then Mona and Nick were upon me as they politely wished me a happy Easter and pried the boys away from me.*

*I'll never forget Kelly's look as he was being taken out of my arms. His lower lip started quivering, betraying his sadness at our parting, and his eyes locked with mine as he was led away, looking over his mother's shoulder, straining to see me. He started protesting and crying, calling out my name. Then, like waking from a daydream, they were gone.*

*The next day, when I ran in to my ex-mother-in-law, she told me that when they brought Kelly to the car, he kept calling out my name and looking for me out the window.*

I wouldn't see the boys again until over a year later, when I was getting ready to move back to the States, where I had accepted a teaching position at a college in Washington state. I had asked Mona if I could see the boys one more time before I moved and, much to my surprise, she agreed, as long as she could be present as well.

The last day I would see the boys was June 27, 2000. It had been a particularly rainy, cold, spring. It seemed every day that summer was dreary and overcast. But that day at the park, the sky was blue, the sun was out, and it was warm. I was so excited to see the boys, it hardly mattered that Mona was there to "supervise." (God forbid I spend any alone time with the boys!) I brought my dog, Aura, a golden retriever. Kelly went directly to her and promptly got a face washing from all of her licking. Kelly had always loved Aura, and Aura seemed quite fond of Kelly.

We spent a couple hours in the park playing on the slides and monkey bars and swings. There was so much laughter and giggling. I was amazed how much they had changed over the last 13 months. When I had last seen them, they had one- and two-word responses. Now they were stringing together short sentences. The more we played, the more they warmed up to me, the more they remembered.

Soon we were off to McDonalds for lunch and play. By this point, I had Kelly sitting on my shoulders with Aura close in tow, about 100 yards ahead of Mona and Ryan. I told Kelly how much I missed him and he replied, "I missed you too, Daddy, I missed you too."

I almost froze in my tracks because this would be the first time (and the last time) in my life that I would ever hear the word *Daddy* referring to me by one of my boys. Tears started streaming down my cheeks as the reality of the moment hit me. I was in a state of wonder, amazed that after all this time Kelly would remember me as "Daddy" and would have the words to express it.

It was over all too quickly, and I found myself waving to the boys in a McDonald's parking lot as their station wagon sped away. Aura and I looked on until the boys disappeared from view and the sun began to set.

# My Own Private Idaho

*We are each other's angels*
*We meet when it is time*
*We keep each other going*
*And we show each other signs . . . .*

*"We Are Each Other's Angels" by Chuck Brodsky*

Riding a bicycle across the country provides a whole new lens on how you see and experience the world as compared to being encased in steel and glass in a passing car. One of the first nights in Idaho, I camped for the evening down in a steep, narrow canyon. My tent was perched in a serene setting next to a young sapling on the banks of the Salmon River. I had just finished eating my dinner and was sitting outside my tent as I wrote of the day's events in my journal. I was dozing on and off, basking in the warmth of the last hours of sunlight, thankful that the day's ride was done. The campground was full of RVs and other people car camping. The river was calm and the air was still. People were throwing Frisbees® as the scent of burgers and hotdogs on the grill wafted across the canyon while young children played and laughed in the distance.

Suddenly, like someone threw a switch, storm clouds formed in the sky above the canyon and it got dark and still. Soon a strong wind came funneling down the canyon and rain came pouring out of the clouds with accompanying lightning, hail, and thunder. The storm caught everyone by surprise, as campers scurried to their cars and RVs, rushing for cover. Then I witnessed something I had never seen before. The wind that came rushing down the canyon soon formed instant whitecaps on the river. Within moments of the storm engulfing us, a thin tree snapped and fell near my tent. I rushed to the cover of my tent, thankful I was inside, and glad my weight created enough ballast to keep my tent from being launched into the river. Then the wind would shift 180 degrees and the whitecaps on the river would come from the opposite direction, with lightning and hail stones coming down all around me. This went on for about the next half hour, with wind shifting from one direction to the other. I never felt so naked and exposed in a storm in my life! The only thing I could clutch on to was my tent and my bike. But as quickly as it had begun, the storm stopped. I was relieved that I was alive and in one piece. I was also quite envious of all the other campers who found refuge from the storm in their own vehicles.

Idaho is known as the Gem State. It is the 14th largest state by land area, bigger than all of New England. It borders six states and one Canadian province and became a state in 1890.

Reflecting on my trip, the most difficult moments involved people, and the most unexpected joyful moments also involved people. In Idaho, one of each happened to me.

Idaho is a mountainous state, and one of the most beautiful I have seen. It has the most designated wilderness land of any state in the lower 48. It also is a desolate state with few people outside of the major cities of Boise and Coeur d'Alene. I entered Idaho across from Ontario, Oregon and then proceeded northward up Highway 95, cutting across toward Montana on even smaller Highways 13 and 12, toward Lolo Pass from Grangeville, Idaho. Once leaving Grangeville, there were no more shoulders as the road became considerably narrower. I was in the midst of what some call the Appalachia of Idaho, meaning I was entering one of the poorest areas of Idaho and also the least populated, with vast stretches of wilderness before me.

The road had me concerned because I was riding a fully loaded bike with no shoulder, making me feel quite vulnerable as I tried to stay a few inches to the right of the white line on the road. I took solace in the fact that the road was not well traveled. I would see the occasional logging truck fully loaded, but thank God, they were always headed towards Grangeville on the other side of the road. I dreaded having one of those trucks fill my side view mirror coming up behind me on my side of the road.

I was coming in to the "big" town of Lowell, Idaho (population less than 500) at the end of what had been a particularly dreary, overcast day, punctuated by a couple of rain showers. For me, it was quitting time around 4 p.m., when about a mile out of Lowell I heard the sound of something all too familiar coming up from behind me. Much to my chagrin, a logging truck, fully loaded, with probably the last load of the day, was barreling up behind me, filling the whole lane that I happened to be in. It was belching exhaust like a fire-breathing dragon, and coming up on me all too quickly. What I had most dreaded and feared was now on top of me, ready to swallow me up.

I was hoping that the driver would jut out into the other lane quickly to get by me, when all of a sudden, rush hour traffic coming from Lowell—three or four widely spaced cars—started appearing on the horizon in that other lane. Instead of going around me, the logging truck driver jammed on his air brakes and started gearing down quickly, trying to avoid creating road kill featuring yours truly and my bike.

Soon he was right behind me as he grinded on his brakes. The smell of burning brake pads assaulted my senses as the air turned black from his belching exhaust. If he got any closer, I could sit on his bumper. Clearly, he was in a hurry to get around me, but felt trapped by the oncoming traffic and so lurched behind me in a glacial pace, awaiting any opening to get around me. Finally, after what seemed like an interminable amount of time and perhaps a quarter mile, he sped up and went around me. I was relieved that this fire-breathing behemoth of a truck was finally around me and gone from sight . . . or so I thought.

Only a mile ahead, there was the logging truck parked off to the side and the driver standing up, facing out in my direction, blocking my path into Lowell, hands on his hips, then motioning me to the side. As I pedaled closer, my worst nightmare came in to focus; he was wearing a tattered, green, faded John Deere baseball cap, and a black muscle shirt (with the sleeves ripped out). His jeans were faded and dirty, with occasional stains from tobacco chew. He had a dark, black moustache with 3-day-old stubble covering the rest of his face. He was clearly angry and I was the object of his rage.

I stopped my bike more in wonderment than fear, too tired to try and pedal around him, thinking to myself, "What the heck is this?" He proceeded to invade my space, and got close enough to my face that I could smell the Copenhagen chew on his breath as he began to scream and yell at me, his spit flying in my face, expressing his indignation for my taking up the road. I stood in stunned silence as if watching a movie of myself, wondering if this really was happening.

My adrenaline quickly awakened me from my momentary stupor as he scoffed at me. "Who the fuck are you, biking on this road?" He jutted his extended finger into my face. "I should have just squashed your fucking bike with you on it. Didn't you see me?" Not waiting for any further reply, he bellowed, "Why didn't you just park your bike on the side of the road and let me through? I should just beat the shit out of you now and get it over with!" Somehow, words found their way out of my fatigued body as I uttered something to the effect of wanting no part of fighting him, since I had pedaled about 80 miles that day and was only in the mood for something to eat and a good night's sleep. I apologized for "inconveniencing him," and I'm sure he saw my deformed left hand. Thank God, he stepped back and broke off his clearly one-sided, heated exchange. I felt like yelling, "Hey, Bud, take a knee," but I restrained myself and said nothing. Of course the testosterone part of me wanted to say, "You want to go? Let's go." But thankfully that part of me became quite muffled, wrapped in my own fatigue. Montana was suddenly looking a whole lot better to me!!!

I encountered many things out West that I had never seen before, having grown up in the Midwest: the Continental Divide, mountain passes, logging trucks, and cattle guards. Cattle guards, like the name implies, show up on roads as a way of impeding cattle going any further down the road. The road is interrupted by a metal grate with intermittent horizontal spacing across the road large enough to break the ankle of cattle that may dare run across. Usually cattle guards are marked by a yellow sign for oncoming traffic, warning of what's ahead, followed by a rumble strip, in case half-dozing motorists miss the sign. Typically, there are white lines framing the upcoming cattle guard giving you final verification. Like I said, usually these are well marked . . . except in Idaho.

My final day in Idaho was framed by low lying clouds that occasionally spit out rain, and again the temperatures were cold and damp, hovering in the low 50s. Something did not agree with me from the night before, because I found myself continually biking in a state of nausea. My stomach was in a knot, convulsing and churning well past the noon hour. Intermittently throughout the day, the nausea it would be punctuated by bouts of diarrhea or vomiting, as if I had a minor case of food poisoning. I would just get done vomiting, and bike a few miles, only to then be overcome with diarrhea. The problem was that there was nowhere to stop for the night and wait for the next day, no campgrounds, no towns, and the forest was too thick with underbrush and rock. So, having no real choice, I pedaled on in my misery.

Finally, near the end of the day, I was at my first major pass of the trip: Lolo Pass leading into Montana. I was wet from the intermittent rain, exhausted, and sapped of any energy to bike up this pass. So I did the only thing left to do, I started walking my bike up the pass. My original intent was to bike up every pass, but that notion had died long ago, with my first pass in Oregon. By this point, I didn't think twice when the strain became too much; I just hopped off my bike and begin walking. Passes in the Rockies are like no other passes in the U.S. It is not unusual for passes in the Rockies to stretch 5, 6, 10 miles at 6% to 8% grade before finally reaching the summit. To go from flat to a 6% to 8% grade puts tremendous strain on your body, particularly your legs, not only riding a bicycle up this incline, but a bike loaded with the weight of fully loaded panniers as well. So there I was, at the end of the day, walking up Lolo Pass.

After vomiting on the side of the road, I noticed an old white Ford pickup truck, likely a refugee from the '60s, slowing down, with a middle-aged couple inside. They must have seen me vomiting and in distress, because they pulled off to the side of the road to talk to me. After the angry trucker the day before, two people so kind and caring were a welcome sight. Their names were Bud and Carolyn, and to this day I swear they came from heaven above. Both appeared to be in their early 50s. Carolyn had long black hair with streaks of grey peeking through. Bud had on an old red plaid shirt that seen a lot of mileage. He was balding on top of his head, wearing glasses that were a little crooked on his face, the right lens visibly cracked on the side.

"This is no place to be riding a bike today," Bud said to me as the truck door slammed behind him.

Carolyn chimed in, "You looked like you were hurting there, so we thought we'd pull over and see if you could use a ride."

They offered to give me a lift over the pass, but at that point I was still intent upon biking the entire way across country and explained my dilemma. I was consumed with the notion that I had to be on my bike for the entire ride across America. Then they came up with a novel idea—dangerous, and stupid, and clearly not well thought out, but novel nonetheless. We decided they would tow me on my bike; we would use a much-too-short rope to tie my bike to their truck. The problem with this arrangement (one of many) is that truck brakes are much more responsive and quick to stop than bicycle brakes.

There I was, zig zagging on my bike with my newfound freedom, yelling, "Wheeee" at the top of my lungs, delighting in the ease of my bike going effortlessly up the pass, thinking I was rescued by a couple of angels, as thoughts of hard-earned rest and nourishment cascaded through my mind. The white center line of the road marked passing miles. Good riddance, Idaho. Hello, Montana! My blissful euphoria went unabated for 1, and then 2 miles, until it came to a screeching halt after about 3 miles into my free tow.

Ah, yes, back to cattle guards in Idaho! My angels of mercy, realizing much too late, to my horror, encountered an unmarked cattle guard and slammed on the brakes. An unmarked cattle guard consists of (a) no "Cattle Guard Ahead" warning sign, (b) no white painted markers across the road indicating a cattle guard ahead, and (c) no rumble strip. With a vision of the truck's bumper becoming a permanent part of my facial anatomy, I braked too. Amazingly, like the lyric from an old Arlo Guthrie song, "I avoided the cliff, but slammed in to the wall." I biked over the cattle guard without bending the wheel of my bike, but I slammed into the back of the pickup and cartwheeled over into the bed of the truck. Luckily, nothing was broken (me or the bike), only a flat tire with some broken spokes. Welcome to Montana!!! I was no longer feeling sick to my stomach. That was now replaced by the trauma of having my life flash before me over and over again in my fitful sleep that night, wondering how the hell I survived that anyway!

CHAPTER 6

# A Life of Difference as an Adult

The next day, after making it over Lolo Pass and coming into Montana, I stopped to get some groceries at a local supermarket. I turned down one aisle only to see a little 5-year-old boy staring up at me. Quickly he pointed to his mother and in a loud, terrified voice, as if he was confronting a monster, he blurted out, "Mommy, what happened to his face? Look at his fingers, they're all gone." Out of embarrassment, his mother swept him up into her arms and ushered him away, uttering a quick apology to me as she made her harried exit.

Later that night in my tent, I wrote in my journal about that incident with the little boy. How I wished for once (or is it the millionth time?) I wasn't different. It gets tiring always being reminded of it. But no matter where I go, I am continually reminded of my disabilities. If it isn't a child pointing at me and asking his mother what happened to me, it is the subtleness of adults looking at me a moment longer, trying to sneak in a second glance at my differentness before looking away.

By the time I reached my senior year of high school, I had no self-esteem left. Oh, my parents believed in me, and my brother and sisters too, for the most part. They believed in me, but I could only go so far with that. I so desired that someone outside of my family recognized me, thought I was lovable, thought I was worthwhile, that I even mattered.

In the history of my schooling, outside of being different, there was nothing remarkable about me. I wasn't gifted with great intelligence, I wasn't a great athlete, I wasn't blessed with good looks or a very charming personality. I wasn't a charismatic leader of anything in my peer group. In fact, I remember a line in a song by Seals and Crofts: "I'm still the king of nothing." That seemed to pretty much sum up my life at 17 years old.

And then something remarkable happened.

In the fall of my senior year of high school, I first met her when I walked into a classroom that was filled with beanbag chairs. My teacher went by the name "Gramma" and she was a little waif of a woman, not much bigger than 5 feet tall. She had this warm, engaging smile, with a radiant personality. She had a most gentle spirit that was remarkably positive. People just felt good about themselves being around her. She seemed to always have this perpetual smile, this sparkling essence about her. As though she was plugged into a socket of optimism and love, she exuded joy and peace. She was 45 years old when I met her, but she had the spirit of someone much younger. She always wore the most stylish, elegant outfits, splashed with color. She told me years later that it made up for the 14 years she was a nun in a convent where all they ever wore was black and white.

I took the class, staying with my pattern of taking all things easy in my nondescript academic career. I took pride in massaging my C average, always looking toward classes that required the least amount of work. Gramma's Social and Family Living class fit the bill. I had heard that you graded yourself; you received whatever grade you thought you deserved. There were no tests and minimal work—a perfect fit for me. I hated school and gravitated toward anything easy to pad my academic load.

I found it very odd to be in a room sitting in beanbag chairs that first day of class and have this little woman that I had never met before start reading to us from the children's classic, *The Velveteen Rabbit*. I remember thinking that it was a cute story, but was confused as to why she began each class reading us this book. I mean it wasn't like I was in first grade again. Then on Fridays, we would have our Warm Fuzzy Day where we would gather around a box filled with folded up little notes with our different names on them as Gramma passed them out to the class. Students would write little notes, usually a sentence or two, and sign their name, or sometimes they would send it anonymously. The notes were always positive and affirming and so that's why they were called *warm fuzzies*. I grew to love Warm Fuzzy Day, because it was the one time I felt I mattered, the one time that what was left of my ego (not much) was stroked. I was always surprised when someone made the effort to write me any note at all.

I was beginning to like this class, sitting around in bean bag chairs, hearing Gramma read to us first from *The Velveteen Rabbit*, and when that was done, *The Little Prince*, and getting warm fuzzies every Friday. What was not to like about this? As I paid attention to the stories, Gramma began making connections between the fairy tale-like stories and our own lives. The stories served as a spider, drawing us further into her web of influence. Slowly, I began to understand what the class was all about. The class was really learning about life, about relationships, about what really matters. And I began to drink it up and fully embrace all it had to teach me.

For the first time in my life, I felt I mattered to a teacher. I felt special. Someone actually believed in me. In all my years of school, the only way I felt special was being the class clown and visiting the principal's office. The two seemed to go hand in hand. Outside of being a good reader and a whiz with my multiplication tables, I was unremarkable as a student in every way. Most of the time, I was bored. I hated school. The only thing I liked was my gym classes, because then I earned credits for playing, the one thing I loved to do. I'm sure most teachers were glad to see me go, because my witty, sarcastic mouth would grow old to them after a while. I was never the teacher's pet and never felt special in any way until I met Gramma in my senior year.

She was a most pivotal figure, at a most pivotal time in my life. By my senior year, I had fully bought into the messages the world had pounded into me.

I was ugly, I was unlovable, and I had no self-worth. The world was not a kind and loving place. But in Gramma's class, I became somebody. She didn't see my hand or my crooked face. All she saw was a beautiful human being. In the movie *Avatar*, to greet one another, instead of saying, "Hi," they would say instead, "I see you," meaning "the essence of me sees the essence of you." That's what it felt like being around Gramma. She was that rare person who could look beyond my disabilities and see my essence, see the beauty that no one else bothered to look for. She saw things in me that I never knew existed. It was one thing to get positive messages from my mom and dad and my brother and sisters. But I would always write it off as family—they had to say nice things about me. But Gramma wasn't family. Here was this kid of average intelligence, just getting by, with no self-esteem, with a deformed face and hand, and yet I was special in her eyes. She was the first person outside of my family who thought I was beautiful. She didn't see my deficits, only my assets—assets that were so well hidden, I didn't even know about them.

So began my relationship with Gramma, a remarkable woman I met at 17 years old who has stayed my friend and mentor to this day. She and her late husband, George, and for the past 18 years, her second husband, Jim, have been my family of choice ever since. I have become the son Gramma never had.

It was during my time in Gramma's class that it dawned on me that maybe I was lovable. Maybe I was worthwhile, despite everything else the world had told me. It was almost countercultural to think that I could actually love myself, because so much of what I experienced was that I was anything but lovable. It has taken me most of my life to come to a point of fully loving myself, loving and accepting Nubby and my crooked face. Still today I catch myself falling short of this from time to time, as I seem to have the hardest time smiling into cameras. But the seed of self-love for me was planted by this amazing soul called Gramma. She started the momentum that has carried me a lifetime. Gramma always said to "love many and each the most." With her and her students, we each felt loved and, if it could be possible, each of us seemed to feel that we were Gramma's favorite. The year after I graduated, Gramma won not only Teacher of the Year for the State of Minnesota, but she also won it for the entire nation!

To this day, 36 years later, I still see Gramma and Jim each Sunday for breakfast. We call it our group therapy. I am forever her student and she is my mentor. At 81 years old now, Gramma's body is betraying her, but she still has that glint, that sparkle in her eyes that reminds me of the radiant, ageless soul inside.

I was definitely a late bloomer when it came to dating. Most people start dating in high school. I even transferred from an all-male college, St. John's University, to a predominately female school (4 to 1 girls to guys), the College of St. Scholastica so that I would have a better chance in dating women. But outside of one date my junior year, I never went out on another date until I was 24 years old. That's when I had my first kiss as well.

I had met Margaret while completing my MSW degree at the University of Georgia. She was a year ahead of me, and upon her graduation, she accepted a social work job in Wilmington, NC. We were in a long-distance relationship for a year, and then we parted company as I moved away to another graduate program at Kansas State University, where I ended up meeting Mona.

A couple of years after my divorce, I entered the world of Internet dating. When I first contemplated the whole idea of Internet dating, one of my friends said to me, "You can be anything you want to be on the Internet." Another friend in Vancouver once took out a personal ad and got over 150 women responding to it. He decided to take on the daunting task of going out on a date with each woman. Months later when I caught up with him, I asked him how it all went. He said, "Tom, what I discovered is that a lot of people lie." Nothing came from any of those dates for him.

I entered Internet dating because of no other choice. How does a busy professional meet eligible women? I had tried singles groups at churches but nothing came of that. So I had entered Internet dating with some reluctance. This was not supposed to happen to me. After all, I was a marriage and family therapist; by now I was supposed to have 2.5 kids, and be living happily ever after with my loving wife in suburbia with a white picket fence. But happily ever after had ended at 9 years, and here I was entering my 40s as a single person dating.

Soon I realized why so many people were eligible singles and came from a history of broken marriages or relationships. I felt like

I was in a big leftover bin, the picked-over pile. There were so many people with so many issues out there dating. It felt like the old game we played in first grade where, as soon as the music stopped playing, we all had to scramble for a seat; God forbid you were the one left standing without a seat. It felt like so many people were desperate to be with someone, anyone. This whole world of Internet dating was amazing. There are sites for Asian women, Hispanic women, fit women, and spiritual women, even for people with disabilities! At first, because of my history with difference doesn't equal beautiful, I thought in order to have a chance, I would put a picture of just my profile, the good side of my face. I would get a fair amount of hits with that. After a while, I thought I've got to be more honest, so I began showing my full profile with my asymmetrical face. The result was no interest at all. Soon, I went back to the profile shots. At least in that way, I thought I might have more of a chance.

The hard part was that occasionally a woman would show interest in me. I always struggled with the next step. When do I broach the topic of my face or hand? Usually, after more of a connection had developed, I would take a deep breath and tell them of my differences. Most of the time I would never hear back from them, or I might get this kind of response from a special education (of all people) teacher after I e-mailed her about my disabilities: "Bummer about your hand and face, good luck with that," and I would never hear from her again.

Dating sites should read, "People with disabilities need not apply." There is the illusion of an even playing field, but that's just what it is for people with disabilities: an illusion. Very few people are interested in dating someone who looks different. In all my years of being on different dating sites, I never saw another person with a disability. In one relationship I had for over a year from Internet dating, I found out after the breakup why she always insisted that she made love with me in the dark. She loved my body but hated looking in to my deformed face.

People have no idea how hard a simple smile can be. There was a faculty development workshop in my college on micro-aggressions, (small acts of unkindness consciously or unconsciously perpetrated on one another in our everyday work lives). They had an exercise in which people painted a big, black X on their faces with black magic marker. Then they were supposed to go around throughout their day noticing how people treated them, noting their rudeness, their stares, and how people talked to them. I thought, "This is no exercise for me. I wear that X in the form of my crooked face every day." In the exercise, they have the luxury to wipe off the black X from their cheek at the end of the day and go back to their normal lives. I don't have that luxury. Everywhere I go, every day I live, I am reminded that I am different. How I wish it could be different, but the mirror doesn't lie. I wake up each day to the reminders that I'm part of a minority group I never wanted to be a part of.

When I was a kid, my crooked smile brought so much daily pain into my life. So many fights, so much loneliness, so much isolation, so much angst was caused by my crooked face. The people closest to me, my family and friends, could only imagine what I felt every day. I'm so envious of people that have beautiful smiles and that smile so easily and freely without giving it another thought. Funny, that's the first thing that attracts me to a woman. Does she have a beautiful smile? To this day, *every time I smile,* I'm self-conscious of how crooked and abnormal my smile is. People bug me all the time when they take my picture. "Smile Tom, come on. That's not smiling, open up your mouth and really smile." They have no idea what kind of pain my smile represents. Still, at 54 years old, I have to consciously remind myself to at least open my mouth and have the beginning look of a smile when people take my picture. I still struggle to smile fully in a picture. I know I smile fully and laugh frequently when there is no camera around, but a picture freezes everything. It captures and highlights not my joy, but my past, my pain, and the struggle of the crooked face it represents. How can something so simple, a smile, be so complex?

There is much more to me than my disabilities. If all that people see is my deformed face or birth defect hand, then they are missing out on so much more to me than that. But very few women gave me more than a second look after seeing my pictures on a dating profile.

I'm sure that I've tried to compensate for my hand and face looking so different. Perhaps that's why I became the class clown all those years, or why when I went off to graduate school, why one master's degree wasn't enough. I had to do more; I earned two master's degrees.

In the course on human sexuality that I have been teaching for 10 years now to college students, we examine mate selection and attraction. The one variable for attraction that seems to be recognized across cultures throughout the world is symmetry. The more symmetry you have, in facial features in particular, the more attractive you are perceived to be. This has been verified with study after study cross-culturally. People with high symmetry experience sex earlier, have more sexual partners, experience more infidelity, and experience more sex. I remember seeing that research and thinking, "God I'm screwed!" It explained clearly (and painfully) why so few women to whom I would write notes on my Internet site would ever respond.

I wish I could be more enlightened about my disabilities and offer a more profound perspective. One of the other courses I teach at the college is called Adults with Disabilities. I had a panel of people in my class one semester with different disabilities. The panel was made up of someone who was deaf, a person with cerebral palsy, someone bipolar, and someone with Asperger's. Each panelist would take 5 to 10 minutes to tell their story before we would open it up to the class for questions and answers. One of the students asked the panelists if they would change anything if they had to do it over again. I was amazed when each one of them said they wouldn't change a thing. I thought about what my answer would be if I was on the panel.

If I had a chance to change anything, I would. I would change my face in a heartbeat. I actually had a chance, or what I thought was a real chance, to change my face 14 years ago when I lived in Alberta. I had visited the local hospital to get a mole removed from my leg. The surgeon that performed the surgery on me looked at my face and said, "You know, I think they can fix that." I said, "No way, this is a paralysis from birth. There is no chance you can fix a paralysis." But after much discussion and a few articles he sent me, I was referred to one of his classmates who was a plastic surgeon. In fact, she was head of surgery at St. Paul's Hospital in Vancouver. She was one of a handful of surgeons in North America who had been trained on a new and obscure procedure that could "fix" my crooked smile.

The procedure consisted of taking a nerve from my calf and transplanting it into my face. Then they took a muscle from my thigh and moved it to the right side of my face, in the hopes that the nerve would grow and innervate the muscle, causing an awakening that would create a symmetrical face with a smile that was no longer crooked. I jumped at the chance, especially with universal health care in Canada where there would be no out-of-pocket costs. It was supposed to be a 2-year protocol with two operations and a 90% chance of success. It seemed like a no brainer. I was more nervous going to the dentist than I was going for my facial surgery. I had no doubt this would be a success. Instead, it ended up requiring eight operations over a 6-year period, and it was all a failure. The good thing was that, unlike in the United States, I didn't have to pay anything (at least monetarily) for their failures.

My last two operations on my face took place when I had moved to Spokane. I came to Vancouver for both of my operations and my surgeon, Dr. Van Laeken, felt so badly, she waived both her surgeon fee and operating room fee each time.

To have the operations fail was disappointing. My doctor was so confident and I frequently thought of what my world would be like to no longer have a crooked smile—to be free of so much pain, to not feel so different all the time. I thought how blessed I was to have the opportunity to eradicate a disability; not many people could say they had that chance. With each operation, my hope would build. Maybe this time it all would come together and work. People around me would try to be positive and say things like, "Yeah, I think there is a change this time, I think it's a little better." But in the end there was no change. The crooked face I was born with was still the crooked face that remained as an adult. I sometimes wondered why it all failed, since I was so positive it all would work. I guess that's a mystery that will remain until my dying day. I take some small solace in that now I know I did everything I could to make it better.

# Final Thoughts on Disability

One of my passions in life is cross-country skiing. I've been cross-country skiing since I was 15 years old. It is truly a mystical moment for me to be cross-country skiing by myself, deep in the woods, see the snow caked on the green branches of the pine trees surrounding me, and only hear the sound of the whoosh of my skis punctuating the silence as I glide across the snow in a ballet-like trance on my skis. It is a profound silence in the depth of winter to be on skis, so deep into the wilderness that the silence is stunning. Sure, you can go to silent places in the city, but still, like a small child hiding finally being found out, the silence of the city is always broken by distant dog's barking, a plane flying overhead, or a car passing in the distance.

After all this time skiing, I found out that cross-country skiing is the number one physical activity you can do that combines aerobic workout, strength training, management of lactic acid build up, and caloric burning. I just liked it because it was fun.

I became a Professional Ski Instructor of America (PSIA-Level 1, Nordic) 12 years ago. When I became an instructor, I received my first ski lessons and discovered all the things I was doing wrong as a skier. The good thing was that I was no longer skiing with duct tape.

When I learned to ski as a kid, I would duct tape my left hand—Nubby—to the pole. I didn't have any fingers to hold the pole, which would have allowed me to firmly plant the pole when skiing. So the next best thing was to tape my gloved hand to the pole in an effort to give me some semblance of power and direction on my left side when skiing. This solution was flawed from the start. For instance, when I would plant the pole, I could never fully trust it because I could never fully know where exactly the pole would plant. Sometimes it would land a foot outside my skis, sometimes it would land too far up or too far back from my skis. The point is that I could never count on it landing where I wanted it to land. But it beat the alternative, which was skiing with only one pole.

Then, when I was learning how to skate ski in Alberta 15 years ago, my instructor, who was a physiotherapist, connected me with an orthotics/prosthetics specialist who created a plastic mold that custom fit around my little hand. It had Velcro strips that could tightly strap me in. Then the whole contraption was screwed on to the top of a ski pole which helped me ski more efficiently than ever before.

A few years back, my disability saved me from a $200 parking ticket. At the end of the ski season, in mid-March, it was the last day that the Elm Creek ski area would be open for the season. I live about 50 miles away, and on that particular day, by the time I arrived at Elm Creek, I had to go to the bathroom really bad. Since it was the last weekend of a season that was fast melting away, I was expecting the parking lot to be half full. To my surprise, when I arrived, there was no parking available except for five handicapped parking slots. I had no idea that the United States Snow Shoe Racing Championship was being held at Elm Creek that day. My options were to drive 2 miles away to the overflow parking and wait 10 minutes for a shuttle bus to pick me up and transport me back to the lodge, which would ensure a burst bladder. Or option number two was to take my chances, park in a handicapped parking slot, rush into the bathroom, and rush back to my car in the hopes the cops wouldn't spot me in my 5-minute window of a bathroom break. I chose option number two.

As I came back to my car, the cop was waiting for me. I thought to myself, "What are the odds?" He appeared to be of Hispanic descent, with light brown skin and short black hair standing straight up with a lot of mousse in it. He wore mirrored sunglasses, the kind that had my reflection in them. He had a toothpick coming out of one side of his mouth, and he clasped his large belt buckle with one hand on each side, rocking back on his heels, back and forth. He started in with a series of rhetorical questions that, if answered truthfully, would have gotten me into more trouble.

For instance, he asked, "So, did you know you were parking in a handicapped parking spot?"

I felt like saying, "Really, I had no idea I was in a handicapped parking spot," as the big blue and white sign with the handicapped parking emblem stood with the words "$200 fine" directly in front of my parked car. "What, you think I'm stupid, of course I saw the sign." Instead, I said, "Yeah, I know, Officer, but I really had to go to the bathroom and I didn't think it would be a big deal to stop in real quickly to use the restroom and then move my car."

He replied, "Oh, so you did know it was handicapped parking and there was a $200 fine, but you chose to park here anyway."

Again, the sarcasm inside of me welled up to the surface and I so desperately wanted to say, "No shit, Sherlock, but what did you want me to do, urinate in public or go to the overflow parking, wait in line, and pee in my pants?"

So without waiting for any kind of reply, he stated, "So that little bathroom break is going to cost you $200. I'll need to see your license." The whole irony of the situation is that in all my years of cross-country skiing, I'm the only instructor I've ever seen in cross-country skiing that has a disability, and in the 8 years that I have skied at Elm Creek, I never once saw a single soul park in any of the handicapped parking slots.

As I reached into my breast pocket to find my wallet, an amazing thing happened. The cop caught sight of my little hand, Nubby. As soon as he saw my hand, his tone changed completely. "Hey, Man, I didn't see your hand. Did you forget your parking sticker?"

Seeing my out right away, I went with his line of thinking. "Yeah, I must have left it a home." Of course I've never had a handicapped parking sticker in my life!!!

With that, he let me off the hook. "Well, here, don't sweat it." He obviously had no clue that I never qualified for a handicapped parking sticker; he just assumed it. "Just park over there, and good luck in the competition. Remember to bring your sticker next time."

I took a big sigh of relief, thanking him, and then thinking, "What competition? I'm not here to snow shoe, I'm here to ski! Way to go Nubby, way to get me off the hook!!" This had to be one of the few times in my life where my disability was actually an asset.

I have come to think how wonderful repression can be. In these pages, I've only given a sample of what I experienced growing up different. There are many other things that happened to me that remain just on the other side of consciousness. My sisters and brother remember other things that I have not spoken of here, things that may forever remain repressed from this story of my life.

The stares from others that I faced as a child I still face today. Adults are more subtle in their stares, but they still stare. The stares still follow me wherever I roam, but I understand better now and accept it. I too would stare, or at least sneak a second look, if someone looked unique or different like me. The novel always invites a second look. I don't judge people for those second looks anymore. I'm much more forgiving now.

My disabilities have been a source of great pain, and provided many challenges to me in my life. I often wondered how my life, my character, would have been different without them. For instance, would I have dated more, been more popular with the ladies? Would I have been a better athlete, stronger, had more endurance? I have no doubt my life would have been a lot easier. And I certainly don't wish my disabilities on myself or others, but I do believe they have been some of my greatest teachers in helping me to continually strive to become a more awakened, loving soul.

# My College Years

Twenty-eight years after I went on my bicycle trip across the United States, I found myself celebrating my 50th year on the planet by going on another epic bicycle trip. This time I was taking the train to East Glacier National Park, where I would ride 1,300 miles, solo again, from Glacier into Alberta and British Columbia, up into Banff and Jasper National Parks, before making my way back down to Spokane, where I would take the train back to Minnesota.

In my trips on my bicycle, there were mostly two kinds of people I ran into as my fellow travelers on spoke-filled wheels. One was students who were usually on some break or convenient pause in their lives before entering their chosen profession or embarking on a graduate degree in a particular field. The other people I ran into most often were teachers, which makes sense, as they may be the only profession that gets summers off.

The funny thing is that I never intended to become a professor. If truth be told, I hated school! I was very sickly as a kid, and so in my first 5 years of school, I missed so much that passing to the next grade was always questionable. Of course with all that illness, I got good at faking sickness as well. For instance, when we moved to Minnesota, I would always come down "sick" during the State High School Hockey Tournament in the first week in March, so that I could stay home and watch the first few rounds of the tournament that were held on Thursday and Friday during the school day.

That was actually quite a sacrifice on some level, because being home sick in my house was not a vacation. If you were sick, with my mom, that meant drinking gallons of water, taking innumerable vitamins, followed by the worst tasting medicine you could imagine, and eating nothing fun or remotely good tasting. The highlight of the menu was saltine crackers and it went downhill rapidly from there.

Outside of spending most of my early years in school catching up because I was perpetually behind from having so many sick days, I hated school; it was so boring! I enjoyed reading, gym, and recess (and I was a cracker jack with those multiplication tables), but that was about it. I lived for summer vacation because I could play all day and not have to go to school.

Because I lacked motivation, I was an intellectual lightweight when it came to academics. For some reason, I was naturally good with history but all other subjects were a struggle to me. I had zero motivation to apply myself. I always did enough to just get by. It helped that I had parents who rarely asked to see a report card. I based my registration for courses on classes that had an "easy" reputation. I prided myself in graduating from high school without ever taking a humanities course, or chemistry, physics, or a foreign language course. In a class of about 800 students, I came in about 400th. There were no honor rolls for me.

In retrospect, I gained nothing academically from my years in high school. High school was just a way station on my way to college. I graduated having no idea how to write a paper, read a textbook, or study for an exam. But not all of my high school years were a loss. I became a better soccer player (our team went 6 weeks without anyone scoring on us, and we finished 6th in the state my senior year), and my tennis game improved slightly playing on the junior varsity team.

To my surprise, I was accepted at both St. John's University and the College of St. Thomas. As I recall, I believe one or both schools accepted me on academic probation. I was set to go to the College of St. Thomas when my parents purchased me a trunk for my high school graduation gift and hinted strongly that "St. John's would be a better fit for you." Each of my sisters and brother received a trunk as a graduation gift from our parents—subtle message? Off to Collegeville I went with my trunk. What a great name for a university town, Collegeville. I think with my undiagnosed ADHD, my parents were happy to see me vacate the nest, and give them some much needed peace and quiet, as I was the last of four kids finally launched.

At 17 years old, I found myself at Mary Hall, a freshman residence hall at St. John's University, an all-male college. In the 1950s, Mary Hall had the distinction of having had a cow snuck up the elevator and let loose on the third floor for fun. Each floor had either a brother or a priest living in an apartment on the premises. Father Robert McGraw (we affectionately called him "Padre" or "Quick Draw"), a philosophy professor, was the priest in residence on our floor. He was a gentle, most compassionate soul, a brilliant man. He gave the priesthood a good name. However, he wouldn't know a marijuana plant from an azalea.

There were more illegal drugs on my floor than what you might find on Hennepin Avenue in downtown Minneapolis. The dealers were known by their nicknames, which is ironic, since I don't remember more than two or three guys from that floor, but I still remember the names of the known dealers living on the premises over 30 years later: "Stoner," "Bong," "Weed," and "Drugs." During breaks like Christmas or Spring Break, many of the residents growing pot plants in their rooms would bring them to the good Padre's apartment to see if he would water them and take care of them while they were away on break. Quick Draw was very proud of himself in keeping those pot plants alive, much to the delight of residents coming back from break. Padre was known to have a "real green thumb."

My roommate that first year was Greg Filbert, a rich kid from an affluent suburb north of Chicago. This kid was so rich that he claimed he never had to make his bed in his entire life; servants made it for him. He was a complete slob; I did teach him how to make his bed. His way of studying was to crank the stereo volume to ten, put on his headphones, and play air guitar while reading his Biology 101 text. I quickly learned that if I was going to study anywhere, it wouldn't be in the room with Guitar Hero playing phantom drums to a Boston album.

I learned more about studying in my freshman year at St. John's than I did in the previous 12 years of public education. Fear is a wonderful motivator. At St. John's, I was in a continual state of anxiety, fearing I would be exposed any moment for the imposter I felt like. Most of the guys attending St. John's came from prestigious, private high schools where many achieved academic honors that far surpassed anything I had done up to that point. In third grade, I did win a school essay contest on "Why My Dad is the Best Dad in the World," but that would prove to be the pinnacle of any academic notoriety I would achieve up until college.

It is a wonder that I write anything at all after surviving the trauma of freshman English. When I decided to attend St. John's, I had the mistaken notion that the brothers and priests in the Benedictine Order would be mostly meek, compassionate, sensitive souls, ready to support and nurture me on the road to higher academic success. Father Robert McGraw certainly fit my stereotypical image of a priest. However, the brother who taught freshman English was quite a departure from this stereotype. In fact, he didn't come remotely close. (That his name escapes me may be repression, which they say is a defense mechanism that may on some level help preserve some of my mental health.)

I remember him being a rather large, rotund man with his black monk outfit making him look even more imposing. He wore the typical white tassel rope belt and hood to complete his black ensemble. He had dark red hair, parted to the side, with a full beard and black, geeky looking glasses. He didn't look like he missed too many meals. I got the sense that he was teaching freshman English out of penance and not some great desire to help us become grammatically literate.

In making my living today as a professor, I was taught early on to never mark a paper in red ink because it was considered "the color of shame." So I mark my papers today in blue, black, green, and sometimes even purple ink, but never red. My professor of freshman English never got the memo on red ink equaling shame. My essays dripped shame. I dreaded getting my papers back from him. There would be more red ink from him correcting my paper than the black ink I used to type it. The only thing he didn't seem to correct was my name on the paper.

In an old Peanuts cartoon strip, Peppermint Patty is sitting at the desk in a classroom and she says to Charlie Brown, "I wonder what my teacher thinks of my paper?" Just then, an essay crumpled into a paper ball floats into her lap, as she states, "I guess he didn't think too highly of it." That cartoon strip pretty much captures about how I felt around my freshman English professor.

After surviving freshman English and my first year of college, I took a year off and transferred to the coed College of St. Scholastica in Duluth. I knew St. John's wasn't the right fit for me about the time guys on the third floor snuck in some porn films and pointed the projector downward to show the films on the snow drifts outside the student union. It created quite a stir as students would look up from the pool table and see *Debbie Does Dallas* outside the windows of the Union on the abutting snow drifts with naked women doing very suggestive sexual moves with their partners. It makes me wonder if these kinds of things happen more often in all-male schools.

Hard to imagine, all those years back at St. Scholastica that I would make a career out of essentially speaking in public as a professor. At St. Scholastica I was a timid, insecure, shy student, who lived in dread of any public presentation I might be required to do for a class assignment.

Going to St. Scholastica was an incredibly rich experience for me. My brother, who is 4½ years older than me, had decided to come back to college for another degree and so he was my roommate my first year at St. Scholastica. I had always put him on a pedestal because he was my big brother. At St. Scholastica, living with him and sharing some of our classes together, I came to know my brother in new ways. He became my equal and I no longer put him on a pedestal. We were practically inseparable.

Both of us took a ballroom dance class, and I felt bad for any of our partners. We both thought we were the better dancer of the two of us. So a woman would be dancing with my brother only to have me cut in and say to my brother, "I'll take it from here," as I strutted my stuff. Then later in class, my brother would do the same to me, and cut in on my partner, showing off his own dance moves. We thought we were legendary, when in reality, the only legends on the dance floor were in our imagination.

My junior year at St. Scholastica, I went out for the soccer team. I wanted to prove to myself that I could play at the next level. I hadn't played since my senior year in high school and since that time, I had grown five inches and put on about 25 more pounds. I played a position my high school coach had thought I would never be able to play: fullback. I wasn't a starter at the beginning of the season, but I had my big break when we went up to Thunder Bay in Canada for a two game series with Lakehead University. I had a bad case of diarrhea and stomach flu, but when the coach told me on the trip up that he was going to start me, I told no one how sick I really was. This was my big chance and I wasn't going to blow it.

I was given the task of marking the current top scorer in all of Canadian college soccer. My team lost both games, but I held their stud scorer to no points for the entire weekend. I frustrated him so badly with my tight marking that near the end of the second game, he was issued a yellow card for purposely kicking me. I spent the half-time of each game in the porta-potty, vomiting and dealing with bouts of diarrhea. That series cemented me in to the starting lineup for the rest of the year. I played my best soccer ever, but I couldn't stand the team.

There were guys on my team who were so panicky and anxious at the start of games that for the first few minutes, if I had the ball, I refused to pass to them because I knew they were so hyper that they would most likely make a dumb play and lose the ball. For road trips, I would always volunteer to drive the van. I wanted no part of hearing their inane, boring, immature conversations, always centered on their next opportunity to get drunk and their latest sexual exploits. When I got back from studying abroad in Ireland, I found out that I was voted Most Valuable Defender for the team. But because I was studying in Ireland at the time, they gave it to someone else; so much for a classy move.

My semester studying abroad in Ireland was the highlight of my years at St. Scholastica. One of my goals in attending college was to find a way to spend a semester studying and living outside of the United States. During my junior year, St. Scholastica launched its first study abroad program, in Ireland. We sent 25 students and two professors to the Republic of Ireland. In many respects, it was ideal. We studied Irish history, Irish literature, religion, and mysticism 4 days a week, and then toured Ireland as a group on a bus 3 days a week. It was amazing to study William Butler Yeats and then view his birthplace later that week.

We stayed in a small town called Louisburg, which was situated on the west coast of Ireland in County Mayo. The town had the distinction of being named after the New World town of Louisburg in Nova Scotia, Canada. Apparently, the Irish settled in Louisburg in Nova Scotia but did not like it there, so they returned to County Mayo and renamed the town Louisburg. Only the Irish would do that!!!

Louisburg was a small, rural town of less than 400 inhabitants on the green rolling hills of the Irish coast. The way of life was far different from anything I was used to in the United States. For instance, there weren't big billboards advertising everything from dog food to banks. There were no big supermarkets. Shopping for food each day was a social event. You made the rounds of visiting the butcher, bakery, and vegetable market. It was not unusual to come to a store that was supposed to open at 9 a.m., only to have the owner show up at 9:20 a.m. and say, matter-of-fact, "Bessy (her cow) took a little longer to milk today" as she greeted you with a warm smile, "What can I do for you today, Darling?" In the States, we would have been livid having to wait around for 20 minutes for a store to open up, but in Ireland it seemed a way of life.

It took me a while to get used to the slower, more deliberate way of life in rural Ireland, but I often think back on those days and miss the pace at which the Irish moved. We lived only a half mile from the sea in traditional thatched roofed Irish cottages. At night, we would frequently leave our windows open, letting the cool breeze blow in as we fell asleep to the sounds of the waves crashing in the distance.

I had no business going to Ireland. If they had known how little money I had, they never would have let me make the trip. This trip was made for students who had much more money than I had. Each week when we would go on tour, we would stay at expensive hotels or beautiful B&Bs. Students would purchase endless supplies of Irish linen, Irish crystal, and Irish knit sweaters. None of this could I afford, and none of it interested me. So I did the next best thing, I camped.

I brought with me a two-person, leaky tent that became my nylon hotel. When we would arrive at a B&B or hotel for the evening, while the group was busy checking in, I would find out when we were going to meet the next morning, and then head out with my backpack for the nearest field or campsite I could find. My classmates would ask me, "So, where you going tonight, Tom?" and I would reply, "Well, I'm thinking of heading north tonight; I camped out on the west of town last night. I've got a good feeling about going north tonight." And then I would disappear into the darkness.

This allowed me to see a slice of Ireland not found in the travel brochures. Because I would set out on my own, no longer as part of a big tourist group, or in little cliques, I would run into the homeless, beggars, and the occasional gypsy. My experience of Ireland was a bit more diverse than drinking Guinness in pubs each evening and buying overpriced souvenirs in tacky tourist shops. In Ireland, I lived the best quote I heard in all of my years in college: "Don't ever let school get in the way of your education."

Going to Ireland was not a very practical or logical decision, but it was most definitely the right decision. I had learned by this time that practical or logical doesn't always equal right. If I had always done the practical thing to do, or what the right thing to do, I would never have gone on my bike trip across the United States 2 years later.

I managed to more than survive Ireland, and I even graduated from St. Scholastica with honors. I've never been big on ego, because I have found that people with big egos are usually connected with great arrogance as well—not a great combination. But I must indulge my ego for a moment. It was great to go home and see some of my classmates from high school who were all honor students and compare GPAs and see that I, Mr. 400 out of a class of 853, Mr. Irrelevant in my graduating class, had a higher GPA in college than most of them.

I did what most people do with a major in psychology; I went to graduate school. Years later I found out that psychology is the number one fallback major for people who have no idea what to major in. While I was in my master's program studying marriage and family therapy, I got an inkling that I might want to teach. In order to teach as a graduate student at Kansas State University, you had to take a course on college teaching. It may have been the most practical course I ever took.

The whole course focused on the methodology of teaching; how to put together a syllabus, creating valid tests, preparing lectures, and videotaping our class presentations. By this time, I had moved through my fear of speaking in front of others. I received great feedback and encouragement from my professor and classmates as well. Years later, I found out what a blessing it was that I had taken this class, since almost all of my colleagues teaching at a college level never had a class on how to teach. Most of them learned their craft through trial and error. Most college professors know their discipline quite well, but have had little to no instruction on how to go about teaching it. That's why I can say that in three degrees and 9½ years of higher education, I had less than five professors I consider to be excellent instructors.

CHAPTER 9

# Teaching

The desire to try teaching wasn't a thunderbolt bursting through the heavens with a loud voice commanding me, "Thou shall try teaching." It was more like a gentle breeze blowing on the back of my neck, a whisper that kept bugging me to try it. When I broached the topic of teaching an undergraduate course to my professors in marriage and family therapy, they were perplexed. Their response was, basically, "Why do you want to try teaching when you're almost done with your training as a marriage and family therapist?" They told me that I was a good therapist and that I should stay with that and not venture off in to teaching.

But the whisper wouldn't go away, and only became louder. So in my last semester of graduate school, I taught an undergraduate class called Human Relations and Sex Roles at Kansas State University. I loved the experience! I loved it so much that upon graduation, I promptly sent out 66 vitas to various colleges across the United States advertising for instructors. One by one, I eventually received 66 rejections.

I let go of the dream for the next 5 years, as I worked on the artistry of becoming a therapist, until the dream was re-awakened when Mona and I had moved north to Prince Thomas, Alberta. It should have been an omen that this might not be Alberta's finest when I found out that the original name for Prince Thomas was Pig Thomas. This was a lumber/mill town, and like most towns in Alberta, Prince Thomas was built in a valley, where the Thompson and Bow Rivers met. The amazing thing is that this place had air quality index warnings because of the air pollution spewing out from all the mills around town. The stagnant polluted air would hover over the valley, creating an epidemic of breathing difficulties and asthma in the region. Here we were, 500 miles away from any metropolitan area, and we had air quality pollution that was worse than Los Angeles. And this was the cleaned up version! Apparently, it had been much worse in the '80s. It was not unusual to come out to your car at the end of the workday and have a thin layer of pinkish tan, thickened dust or powder caked on your car from debris blowing around in the air from the pulp mills further up the valley.

The Dawson Lake college in Prince Thomas was my first opportunity to teach full time at a college. They had a grant-funded, experimental program called Basic Mechanical Training (BMT), in which we trained ex-convicts how to become car mechanics while I was to teach them life skills.

I can't think of a tougher group for your first formal, full-time teaching experience than the "BMT boys." The class was all males, and each had done prison time for charges ranging from assault and battery, to armed robbery, to attempted murder. Clearly they were in the class for mechanical training and NOT life skills. It didn't help that my class came at the end of the day, from 3 to 5 p.m., after they had been working on cars all day.

That first day of class they came in late, strolled to the back of the room, far away from me, slouched in their chairs, and folded their arms across their chests. Their basic attitude was, "So, what are you going to teach me?" They had come right in from the shop, in dirty, grease-stained, grey overalls. They came with no pens or paper and showed zero investment in the process. Two things became clear right away: (1) they did not think they needed any life skill training, and (2) they had no idea what life skills were all about. It became obvious from that first moment that any hope that this group would openly receive and see the relevance of the information I had planned to impart was futile. I quickly went to Plan B; I just had to figure out what Plan B was. The quote from *The Wizard of*

*Oz* was ringing in my ears about then; "Toto, I don't think we're in Kansas anymore!"

Clearly, they were not ready for any classroom experience. I felt like I was in front of a group of middle school students in detention, not adults. So I decided to treat them as if they were my case load. I operated from the assumption that "I don't care how much you know until I know how much you care." I concluded that I needed to get to know them as individuals, so I decided to meet with each one of them individually over the next few months—my version of divide and conquer. I would take them to coffee, shoot pool, meet one-on-one in my office, or go shoot some hoops.

I would start out by asking them safe questions like, "What's your favorite color?" I discovered their favorite colors were either black or blue. I thought to myself, "Isn't that great, the color of bruises." They all described themselves as "easy going." I thought to myself, "I'm easy going until you piss me off." One of the guys who called himself easy going told me how he was ready to kill a guy over a drug deal that had gone bad. He had had him in the sight of his rifle but he decided at the last second to "just wing him." After that, I wanted to make sure I was always on his good side; I didn't want to get "winged' in the parking lot some day for giving him a bad grade.

I survived my year with the BMT boys. When an opening for an instructor in the Human Services Program at the college came open the next year, I applied and was accepted. This launched my college teaching career over the next 20 years and counting, in two countries, two states, teaching at community college, 4-year baccalaureate colleges, and graduate school programs.

I think my favorite level to teach at is the community college level. Why do I say that? A story from India called "The Chicken and the Eagle" may illustrate. As I've heard it, the story goes something like this:

> A baby eagle (eaglet) was orphaned and grew up in
> a backyard chicken coop with chickens. It did as the
> other chickens would do; it would cluck and cackle

and fly a couple of feet in the air and walk around the chicken coop all day. One day, the eaglet was sitting by the barnyard fence with an older chicken when he looked into the clear blue sky and saw a magnificent bird soaring with its wings outstretched above. He looked up in wonder and asked the elder chicken, "What kind of bird is that?" The older chicken replied, "That's an eagle, the king of the sky, but we could never be like that. We're chickens and we can only fly a few feet." So the eagle grew up and lived in the chicken coop for the rest of his life never realizing that he, too, was "the king of the sky." He died thinking all along that he was a chicken, when in reality, he was an eagle.

I wonder how many of us never realize our magnificence. This story reminds me so much of community college students. Like me, so many students have massaged their C average and never put much effort in to school. Or, they may have dropped out for a variety of reasons and gotten their GED. Still others may have done time in prison or spent years abusing drugs. I call my classroom a "laboratory of wonder." I see personal transformation happen on a regular basis right in front of me. In human services, you become the tool of influence. So in the curriculum, you not only learn how to intervene and make a difference in the lives of your clients, but you can't help but grow and become a better version of yourself along the way. Consequently, each day as their professor I am privileged to have a unique perch where I witness students' awakenings. We have to be one of the few programs I know of anywhere that develop not only students' heads, but their hearts as well.

In such programs, students who were told they were dumb or stupid or wouldn't amount to much, that they were chickens, experience their own personal epiphanies and discover that they really are eagles. They find great success in the program and go on to graduate from our program and also earn a bachelor's degree. Some even go on to graduate school. As the author Marianne Williamson once said, "Your playing small doesn't serve the universe." I dare my students to be extraordinary every day, and I see people who were chickens dare to soar and fly for the first time in their lives. It is a most sacred moment to witness an eagle beginning to soar. Now I'm seeing my students going on to get master's degrees and even doctorates. Who knows where their soaring will take them?

The cool thing is that, as a professor at a community college, I get to be a small part of people's dreams, and I love it. I talk about dreams a lot with my students: their dreams. They don't necessarily call them dreams; they usually refer to them as goals. But the only difference between a dream and a goal is that a goal is a dream with a deadline.

My Basic Counseling Skills class is the most experiential class in our program. It is a very intimate class, as well, because students are taught different counseling skills and then they go into labs where each of them takes turns switching from counselor to client as they work at developing their helping skills. Counseling really is an art, a craft. They are instructed to talk about real problems in their lives, not made-up ones, or at the very least, real problems from their past. Consequently, it is a class like no other, in which students get to know each other quite well. At the end of the semester, in putting a final exclamation point to the experience, we go around the room, sharing final words about just how this course has impacted each student's growth as a professional and a person. What students have to say can be quite moving at times. During this circle time, I also give them my final story, paraphrased and embellished greatly from the book by Ed Hays called *Twelve and One Half Keys*. The story from that book that I retell with my students is called "The Stranger's Bargain," and it goes something like this:

> Did you ever go to a movie where you were trans-
> ported to another world? The movie is so captivating
> that you don't want it to end. The credits start ap-
> pearing on the screen, the lights go on, people begin
> crowding the aisles in a hurry to get out, and soon

the cleaning staff is in sweeping up spilled popcorn, and giving you a look that basically says, "Can you hurry up and get out of here so we can all go home?" That was me at the first *Star Wars* movie that came out in the late 1970s. I was attending college and it was a Friday night in Duluth. I went by myself to the late show at 9 p.m. It was a cold, January night in Duluth and there I was, not wanting to leave the movie theatre. By now the screen was black, and I was the last one left in the theatre. As I was ushered out the exit into the night, the dialogue was still running through my head, when Luke Skywalker™ engages Darth Vader™.

By this time, the parking lot was empty, except for a black van that was parked next to my heap of a car in the back of the lot. As I hurriedly bundled up my coat, I thought to myself, "What are the odds that out of a whole empty parking lot, this van would be parked next to my car?" As I got closer, I noticed the driver was out scraping his windows, letting his van warm up, and smoking a cigarette as he zipped up his jacket to combat the cold rolling in off of Lake Superior. I quickly got in to my car, started it up, and jumped outside to let it warm up and scrape the windows free of all frost as well.

Soon, the stranger struck up a conversation with me as he took another drag off his cigarette.

"So, did you come from the movie theatre?"

"Yeah."

"What movie did you see?"

"I saw *Star Wars*." I quickly added, "Did you see it yet?"

"Na," he replied, "I don't like those places."

Puzzled, I asked, "What, you don't like movie theatres?"

The stranger replied, "No, I don't like those places."

I thought to myself, "Are you kidding? How can you not like going to the movies? I love the movies!!! If I could watch movies all day I would."

His obvious disdain for movie theatres compelled me to ask, "What is it about movie theatres you don't like?"

He tapped on his cigarette and folded his arms across his chest. I could see his breath rise from his mouth as he said, "I don't like those places because they are dream factories. People leave their mundane, trouble-filled lives and find a bit of relief in the movies. And depending on the movie, they might begin to awaken from their unconscious stupor and dare to begin to dream again of possibilities for their lives that may have been lying dormant or not even imagined until that moment. No," he said, as he took another drag on his cigarette and inhaled deeply, "I don't like those places at all."

I was intrigued by this individual's peculiar take on movies, and we began to talk more as the time approached midnight. It turned out, to my great surprise, that the stranger in the black leather jacket next to a black van smoking a cigarette was the devil himself! I always thought the devil was a fictitious character that was red, with a bald head, evil-looking eyes, and a pitchfork. This was not the devil I had ever imagined. He looked so plain and unremarkable. "So this is the devil," I thought. "What the heck is he doing talking to me in a parking lot in the middle of a cold night in January in Duluth, Minnesota?"

"So, I suppose you are after my soul?"

He laughed as he paused, propped one foot on his bumper, and looked out into the night sky. "No," he said, as he looked back at me with dark, piercing eyes, "I'm not after your soul. That's old Dorian Gray stuff," he chuckled. "You guys all think I'm after your soul, but really I could care less about that."

"Really," I asked in a surprised tone. "Then what are you after? Surely the devil has got to be after something!"

He said, "No, I'm not after your soul." He paused and then looked right through me, "I'm after your dream. Everybody has a dream. When you are little kids, you all dream about being the famous baseball slugger, or being a model, or a movie star. And then when you get older, those dreams fade, only to be replaced by others—dreams of going to college, getting married, finding a good job. But at some point, usually when people get into their 30s or 40s, usually after they've been beaten down by life, maybe going through a divorce, having a miscarriage, or being fired from a job, people quit dreaming. Oh, they may go through the motions and live another 30, 40, 50 years, but the minute they quit dreaming, I've got them. I'm not after their soul, Tom, I'm after their dreams."

About then, I felt a chill up my spine and a strong need to get away from this creepy individual called the devil. By this time, my car was warmed up, my windshield was clear, and I was ready to go. As I got into my car, he motioned to me to roll down the window as he took another drag from his cigarette. He asked me, "So, what about you, Tom, do you still have a dream?"

I replied, "Oh, you bet I do. I'm sure not going to share it with you, but I've got a dream and it's pretty amazing. In fact, I've got a lot of dreams that I haven't begun to give up on." With that, I rolled up the window and sped off. As he began to fade in my rearview mirror, still with one foot propped on his bumper, looking out at me fading into the quiet downtown of Duluth, the clock at the church just down the alley struck midnight.

I tell my students this story to inspire them to keep dreaming, that no one can take away your dream unless you let them. The minute they lose their dream, the minute they settle, they compromise their soul; they live a life of so much less.

We talk about life a lot, especially in my Loss and Grief class, which I teach about every other year. During the course, I lead them on a meditation, courtesy of my favorite author, Anthony de Mello, in his book of spiritual exercises titled *Wellsprings*. The meditation goes something like this (loosely paraphrased):

> Imagine that you are at your own funeral. Your body is all dressed up in a casket that is open for viewing. Notice who gives your eulogy and what they say about you and this life you lived. Note what kind of day it is; is it sunny or overcast, is it spring time or fall? Then listen to what the minister says about you. You agree with some of the things he says about your life, and other things he says about your life, you ponder and wonder about. You see your loved ones, dressed in black in the first row. Some are crying and some stare blankly out into space. You wonder what they are thinking about as the minister drones on—memories of you, perhaps some focused on some disappointments they had with you, regrets, or momentary thoughts about what's in your will for them.

> You notice the crowd in the church. Some of your colleagues or coworkers are in the crowd. There may even be some in the crowd who aren't that sad that you are gone. They listen silently with their eyes fixed on the speaker in front, as your life of so many years

and so many memories is summarized in a matter of minutes. Some of the teenagers in the crowd are actually texting some friends, completely oblivious to the gravity of the situation.

You are now at your gravesite, the casket is closed, and the people are huddled around as your casket is slowly lowered into the ground. The minister says a final word or two. There is more muffled crying at your gravesite as the crowd files by, each person placing a handful of dirt on your grave as they silently say their last goodbyes. And now you are gone.

A year goes by, and you revisit the world you had left. Your gravestone is still very fresh and new looking, not like the weathered stones up over the hill of those who have gone long before you. There are even some decaying flowers from a few weeks back still lying at the foot of your grave.

You revisit your place of work and you've been replaced. Every once in a while, someone mentions your name in passing, but now someone else sits at your desk and someone else parks in your parking spot.

Since you died a year ago, a couple of neighbors down the block have moved. A young couple moved in with a young child just across the street. They built a new bank next to the gas station you used to fill up at on your way to work. Across the street from the new gas station is a senior citizen assisted living center that just opened up this last week.

Your car is gone. Your niece who just went away to college is driving it now.

Your spouse has repainted your bedroom and finally got rid of the old linoleum in the kitchen that you were going to replace someday but never had time to do so. All of your clothes have been given away to the Goodwill. Your spouse has a picture of you on her mirror, and the family gathered this past June to toast what would have been your 40th wedding anniversary.

Your spouse has a tear or two when holidays come around and she is reminded of your absence. But for the most part, life goes on without you.

Now it is 10 years after your death. You revisit the world you once lived in. Your gravestone is more weathered now; there is even a chip or two missing on the surface. There is a newer gravestone next to yours; it is your spouse's.

At work, your name is never mentioned any more. All the people you once worked with are re-tired now, replaced by younger workers who have no memory of you.

Your house was sold a few years back, after your spouse's death. The trees in your neighborhood are much bigger now, forming a canopy over the street. More of your neighbors have died, retired, or moved away. Your church has a new minister now, a much younger woman, fresh out of seminary. Your grand-children are now all grown up. Your oldest grand-daughter is now expecting her first baby. She has a few pictures of you. She kept all the old family photos you collected in albums over the years. Otherwise, not much is left of you. No one really mentions you anymore except maybe at Christmas or Easter.

Now a hundred years have passed since your death. Your gravestone is now old and weather-beaten. Some of the writing has faded off; the color of your stone is muted. You now are joined by the graves of all of your children nearby.

The company you once worked for is no longer there, having moved out of state 40 years ago. Your house is still there, but four or five families have made it their home and moved on since then. The siding has been replaced twice and the new owners have added a solarium and a pool. There may be a picture of you left stored away in some forgotten trunk, but your name, your memory, are now long gone. It is as if you never existed or lived on this earth.

At this point, I have my students open their eyes and write for a few minutes about what this meditation was like for them. Then I ask them "How many of you know the names of all your grandparents?" Almost all, if not all, of the hands go up in the classroom. Then I ask how many of them know all the names of their great grandparents and only about a quarter of the hands go up. Then I ask, "How many of you know all the names of your great grandparents," and none of their hands go up. Then I tell them to look around, to notice that no one's hands are up.

That's when I say, "See, you are all 100 years from your own extinction. In the arrogance of our temporariness, we think we are so important. We can't imagine the world going on without us, but it does. The world has been going on without us for millions of years and it will continue to go on without us, hopefully, after we are fertilizer and pushing up daisies for another million years. How many times do you mention your great grandma's name, or what do you even know about your great grandfather?"

Most students answer, "Never," or "Very little."

"Your life will be summed up in a sound bite." I ask them, "So what do you want your sound bite to say about you? Do you want to be known as an alcoholic? Will they say 'I don't know much about Grandpa, but he sure was an ornery old cuss!'? Or will they say about you, 'She was a great mother,' or 'He was such a loving, devoted husband.'?" Then I challenge my students by saying to them, "You are creating your sound bite, your legacy, every day. You are the author of your life. You write the story of who you are every moment, every day of your life. Every action you take, every choice you make, is an act of self-definition. So I ask them, "What story are you going to write? What legacy are you going to leave? What sound bite will you create with your life?"

Teaching is my life, my story. The funny thing is, if truth be told, I don't teach my students anything. (Of course, if I had said that at my interview, I never would have been hired.) In the end, I believe we teach ourselves. The students are the ones who decide whether to come to class, the ones who study for the exams, the ones who take notes, and the ones who write the papers. All I do is facilitate their learning, or, as I define education, facilitate their awakening. Hopefully, I inspire students' awakening, incite their passion for the topic, and don't get in the way of it.

I challenge my students to "be the difference that makes a difference" in our client's lives. Be the voice to the voiceless; give hope to those who feel hopeless. Be the weaver of meaning in our client's stories. One such occasion happened shortly after Hurricane Katrina slammed into New Orleans. Our department decided to sponsor a Hurricane Katrina reconstruction trip to New Orleans.

Driving in vans from Minnesota, we came into New Orleans just after 11 p.m. Students who had been sleeping most of the day were now wide awake as we drove toward the Upper Ninth Ward. It had been 10 months since Hurricane Katrina had swept through, leaving in its wake a devastated city just now stumbling to its feet. Most of our students had never been out of the Midwest, let alone ever driven through a disaster zone the size of Katrina.

The city was eerily dark and quiet. As we entered the Upper Ninth Ward, there were no street lights on and most of the houses were dark and abandoned. There was no sign of life, not even a dog barking, and few cars on the street.

We had been on the road for 12 hours that day, well into our second full day of travel from Minnesota. All of a sudden, we almost rear-ended the van in front of mine; I threw on the brakes and my van came to a screeching halt. "What the fuck is going on?" As I looked around at my students, they were already on edge as we inched forward into *the heart of darkness*, to borrow Joseph Conrad's title. Then we slowly started to creep ahead as we veered around a pothole that easily could have swallowed our van. We could have walked faster than our van was moving, as we were constantly veering from one side of the road to the other avoiding massive potholes from engulfing our vehicles. The street looked like craters on the moon, like it had been targeted in some kind of a bombing run. Just then, I remembered what a National Guard member who had served in Iraq said shortly upon arriving in New Orleans: "This looks like another Baghdad, only worse!" Soon we passed one house burning to our left and another house burning to our right. There were no fire trucks on the scene to put out the fires.

Finally, we arrived at our destination, St. Mary's School. There were no lights on, only a woman on the front steps smoking a cigarette. As we poured out of our vans, we heard a gunshot in the distance. That's when I whispered back to my students, "Toto, I don't think we're in Kansas anymore." This was our welcome to New Orleans and the aftermath of Hurricane Katrina. St. Mary's would be our home for the next 7 days as we partnered up with Common Ground, a grassroots organization spearheading the rejuvenation of the Lower Ninth Ward in its recovery from Hurricane Katrina.

It had started out as a vague idea, a nice sentiment among our students in the human service program at Inver Hills Community College shortly after Katrina devastated New Orleans on August 29, 2005. Never did I imagine that 10 months later, my colleague Cheryl Redinger and I would lead a group of 25 faculty and students from our college on a Hurricane Katrina rebuilding mission. Instead, we all watched in helpless horror as each night the television brought us live reports on the devastation of Katrina and the suffering people of New Orleans. We talked about Katrina in our classes, and students periodically implored us with vague requests like, "We've got to do something about this." Quietly, I thought to myself, "Yeah, maybe we can take up a collection and send a check to the Red Cross, or maybe organize a clothing drive."

Then one day, Cheryl came into my office and floated the idea of doing something more, like maybe organizing a student relief trip. (I found out later that she was secretly hoping that I would axe the idea as stupid and unrealistic.) I had only started teaching at the college that semester, having just moved into the area from

Washington State in July. We were just getting to know each other back then as colleagues. Neither of us knew that the other had a long history of "thinking outside the box." Instead of dismissing her idea as preposterous and unrealistic, I surprised myself, and I'm sure Cheryl, when I said, "Yeah, maybe we could do that." Of course neither one of us had any idea of how we were going to pull this off.

The college administration, to its credit, was highly supportive of the endeavor. However, because there was no template for such an adventure, we found ourselves making it up as we went along. This was not a paint-by-number operation. We had to create health forms, liability forms, and so on. Somehow, we put it together well enough so that by the following May we had 25 students and faculty crammed into five minivans pointing south to New Orleans and heading into the great unknown. Like the lyric from the 1970s musical *Paint Your Wagon*, "Where are we headed, I don't know. Where we goin' I ain't certain. All I know is I am on my way!"

The City Council of New Orleans adopted an ordinance in 2006 called "Eminent Domain." This document stated that if property owners hit by the hurricane did not show substantial improvement in repairing their damaged houses, the city could offer them $8,000 for their house and property and take over possession later that year. Some saw this as a veiled, racist way of getting rid of poor people of color and property owners from the Lower Ninth Ward. Early on, our mission became gutting flood-damaged homes filled with mold and water damage as a way of showing substantial improvement, and thus helping poor homeowners keep their homes and avoid the consequence of the eminent domain regulation. When we heard the personal stories of survival from the homeowners for whom we were gutting homes, it became our personal and impassioned mission to help save as many homes as possible in the Lower Ninth Ward.

Gutting a home involves stripping all dry wall and mold-imbedded materials down to the bare walls, leaving only the studs. This involves wearing white Tyvek® suits and oxygen masks while toting crowbars and wielding sledge hammers. The work is very hard, physically exhausting. For instance, it was not unusual for, by lunch break, to have to change into a second t-shirt under my Tyvek® suit because it was so drenched in sweat; it looked like I had dived in to a swimming pool. The temperatures hovered in triple digits with the humidity regularly registering at over 90%. The smell from rotten food in refrigerators and unabated mold buildup from 10 months of sitting in flood damage was nauseating and suffocating.

That first year, we spent most of our time gutting Mrs. Reed's house. The only reason her home survived was because it was a two-story brick structure, the only brick house on the block. The first time I saw her house, I thought it resembled more of a small apartment building than a single family home. Her house was located only a half mile from one of the main breaches of the levees in the Lower Ninth Ward. Mrs. Reed was a proud African American woman in her late 50s who was a former worker in city hall. Her adult son lived in the same house.

We took out so much rotted dry wall and other debris that we created a pile of garbage that went from the ground floor all the way up to the second story window from which we were throwing all the stuff out of her house. At one point, when we were throwing out hundreds of warped and damaged records, Mrs. Reed's son left the house in tears, muttering to us, "Do you realize you are throwing my life out that window?" (He worked as a DJ in a local pub.)

May of 2012 was our seventh year of going to the Gulf region to help with Hurricane Katrina reconstruction efforts. The first 3 years, we worked in New Orleans, focusing predominantly on cleanup efforts in both the Upper and the Lower Ninth Ward, some of the worst hit areas of New Orleans. The fourth year, we went to Plaquemine Parish, which is an extreme southern, rural parish that lost over 80% of its dwellings due to the force of Katrina. The last 3 years, we have partnered up with Habitat for Humanity Gulf Coast in Biloxi, Mississippi in helping with reconstruction efforts in that area.

It has been years since the great deluge of Katrina hit the Gulf in 2005. Sadly, America has moved on and Katrina has become old news. What the vast majority of Americans don't realize is that

Katrina devastated over 90,000 square miles, an area the size of Great Britain. In 2012, there were still over 68,000 uninhabitable homes in New Orleans alone as a result of Katrina. Each year after the trip, Cheryl and I think that will be the last trip to the Gulf for us, only to be pulled back magnetically by the stories of the Mrs. Reeds of the region, and the impassioned pleas of our students to go back and live the motto of our Human Service program: "Be the difference that makes a difference." So once again, next May, with our little convoy of five minivans and 30 students and faculty, Katrina will bring us back down south like migratory birds to once again lend a hand and help to rebuild the region one house at a time.

What I have discovered is that to teach is an honor and a privilege, a calling that I do not take lightly. To teach is truly to touch the future and to invite transformation with my students. I have taught close to 5,000 students now in my 20-year career (and over 3,000 skiing students as a cross-country ski instructor). I hope I have touched them, but I know they have touched me.

There are more than 10,000 lakes in Minnesota. Teaching reminds me of being on the lake shore of a small lake just at sunrise, when the early morning fog is lifting as the first rays of the morning sun pierce the lifting mist. The lake is as still as a mirror, not a ripple to be found. When I teach, it's as though I throw a rock into the glassy surface of the lake and watch the ripples move slowly across to the distant shore. When I instruct students in the field, I create ripples in their lives, and who knows where the ripples end? I have taught people to be social workers or human service workers who go on, because of my instruction, to work with the homeless, domestic violence, foster care, and many other vulnerable populations. The ripples of influence as they intervene with their clients last long after I've become a faded memory. Do they ever really end? That thought and image give me much peace in pondering that perhaps I really did become "the difference that makes a difference."

*Cook family 1950s*

*Oregon starting point*

*Idaho - typical camp site*

*Dillon, Montana*

*Bicycling near Royal Gorge, south of Cannon City, Colorado*

*Chesapeake Bay, Virginia - finish*

*Gramma 2011*

# The Continental Divide— Been There, Done That

*Miles from nowhere, guess I'll take my time, oh yea, but it's alright. Got my freedom, I can make my own rules, the ones I choose. Lord my body, has been a good friend, I won't need it, when I reach the end.*

—Cat Stevens *"Miles From Nowhere"*

As part of our nation's 200th anniversary as a country—our bicentennial, in 1976—a bicycle company in Missoula, Montana, developed maps and accommodation tour book guides for bicyclists biking across the United States in a celebratory event called Bikecentennial. In 1981, when I was planning my trip, they were still publishing these maps and tour guides. I was able to purchase these items and follow their suggested bike route maps, which made planning my trip across the United States that much easier. It felt like paint by number; just get the maps and tour books and away I went!

The author of the tour books wanted to make this the most scenic route possible. Accordingly, the route they chose was anything but a straight line from point A to point B. Instead, they created the most winding route imaginable.

It was in Montana that I first encountered the Continental Divide—the line that divides the flow of water between the Pacific and the Atlantic oceans. On the western side of the Divide, all the water flows to the Pacific Ocean. On the eastern side, all the water flows towards the Atlantic Ocean. The divide runs from northwestern Canada through the Andes mountain range in South America. The divide enters the United States along the crest of the Rocky Mountains in Glacier National Park and follows the Rocky Mountain range through New Mexico.

Between Montana, Wyoming, and Colorado, I crossed the Continental Divide nine times.

At first, coming from the Midwest where there are no mountains, I was excited about crossing the Continental Divide; it wasn't something I had experienced back in Minnesota. But by the time I reached Colorado and hit the Divide for the NINTH time, I was beginning to feel like Bill Murray when he played the weatherman in the comedy *Ground Hog Day*, where every day is the same. At that point in the trip, I was wondering out loud to myself, "Who the heck planned this route?"

I entered Montana through the Lolo Pass on the Idaho/Montana border. This was the route that the Lewis and Clark expedition used on their search for the Pacific Ocean in 1806. Today, this area is known as the Bitterroot Valley of southwestern Montana, about 40 miles south of Missoula.

The state of Montana is the fourth biggest state in terms of area (slightly bigger than Japan) but ranks 44th in population, just under a million people. It is the third lowest state in terms of population density. Over 60% of the state is prairie, with the rest covered by 77 different ranges of the Rocky Mountains. It's anticipated that, because of global warming, all of the glaciers will have melted away in Glacier National Park by 2030. There are seven different Indian reservations in the state, which also boasts the largest grizzly bear population in the lower 48.

I wasn't long biking in Montana when I ran across something I had never seen before. I was on Highway 12 in extreme western

Montana, slowly making my way east toward Dillon, Montana in the southwest part of the state, when I no longer saw the highway ahead of me in the distance. Instead, I saw a sea of brown and white colors bobbing up and down in the distance. I had no idea what it could be. As I got a little closer, I noticed there were cowboys on horses, and that sea of brown and white colors bobbing up and down were cattle, and they were all coming toward me, or at least it seemed that way. There had to be over 1,000 cattle coming in my direction. I had never seen a cattle drive in person before, so this was quite shocking. I kept rubbing my eyes wondering, "Is this what I think it is?" The next question that came to my mind was, "Hmm, how the heck am I going to get through the cattle drive without getting killed?"

I began to feel a knot form in my stomach. It was dawning on me that this might not be a good idea, to continue biking toward that mass of meat and hoofs coming at me in my two-wheel bike with one-and-a-half-inch-wide tires. Just when I was about to turn around and look for an alternative route, a red Corvette appeared out of nowhere, and I knew that would be my ticket in parting this sea of cattle coming at me. I got right on the bumper of the Corvette and we inched our way through the cattle drive with no harm done. I've always loved red Corvettes!

That night I camped in the town of Dillon, Montana, the home of Western Montana University.

About a decade after my cross-country bike trip, I spent the 1990s living in Alberta, and the first 5 years of the new millennium living in Washington state. While teaching in Alberta, I used to get summers off, so I spent a couple summers working in a place called Holden Village running their "Hike Haus" in the Glacier Peak Wilderness Area of the north Cascades. I spent a lot of time in that region, climbing mountains, clearing trails, and leading hikes. In 2000, I moved to Spokane, and spent even more time in the mountains, having joined a local mountaineering club and a backpacking club.

One of the first things you learn if you are going to spend time hiking in the mountains is to always pack the 12 essentials. (Depending on what guide you consult, this has also been called the

"10 Essentials" or the "13 Essentials.") The point is that no matter how mild the weather may seem in starting out on a hike, when hiking in the mountains, no matter what season it is, it's imperative for survival to bring a large day pack equipped with survival gear and extra clothing in case you encounter unexpected inclement weather. Mountains can create their own weather and when you are hiking up in altitude, bad weather can come upon you unexpectedly and you need to be prepared. On more than one occasion when I was running the Hike Haus at Holden Village, we would encounter hikers who would start their hikes in t-shirts and shorts and not bring any additional gear, only to be caught in bad weather a couple hours down the trail, where the temperature might drop 20 degrees in a span of less than 20 minutes, and they would be exhibiting the initial stages of hypothermia. Inevitably, when we would ask them where they were from, they would almost always say they were from the Midwest; and we would shake our heads in disgust and say in unison, "Flatlanders!"

*Flatlanders* is the slang term for people who had never spent time in the mountains; they get caught doing stupid things, like hiking without the 12 Essentials, because they come from places like the Midwest which are close to sea level, and they have never experienced how quickly the weather can turn in the mountains, and how harsh and unforgiving it can be. If you are not careful, this can be a very real danger—life threatening.

In my bike trip across the United States, I too was a true flatlander, and I paid for it. I was obsessed with getting rid of as much "unneeded" weight as possible. The whole state of Oregon was my training state, and I was in constant pain from biking over numerous passes packing heavy weight in the form of loaded panniers on my wheels. One of the ways I occupied my time was racking my brain for ways of cutting down my gear weight to the bare minimum. Believe me, if I could have biked naked, I would have!

At the end of my time in Idaho, I came up with the brilliant idea of getting rid of almost all of the extra clothing I had packed in preparation for this trip. I figured that I was now approaching mid-June, and that winter had to be long gone by now. I decided to box up my down vest, mittens, sweatshirt, wool socks, my wool winter hat, and long pants, because I thought it would be nothing but warm, summer weather from here on out. That certainly would be the case even in the upper midwest of Minnesota. I was so relieved, and my bike felt so much lighter once all these bulky, extra items were boxed up and shipped off at the next local post office. This proved to be the dumbest decision I made on the entire trip.

That night, camping in Dillon, I met up with the first bicyclists I had seen since Oregon. Jeremy and Jason were brothers who were bicycling from Seattle to Dallas. They had been out on the road about as long as I had been. It felt good to share a camp with guys my own age who were on a similar adventure. We talked into the night, sharing stories from the road as they made s'mores around the campfire.

The next morning, I woke up to a saggy tent. I didn't realize how cold it had gotten during the night until I woke up and could see my breath inside my tent. It sounded unusually quiet outside my tent, like the world was muted. I slowly pulled down the zipper on my tent flap and was startled to find out why my tent was sagging; it had snowed a couple of inches that night!!! It was June 16th and I woke up to snow on the ground. As I slowly broke camp, I had fun throwing snowballs at Jeremy and Jason as I pondered what to do next. I was also silently cursing myself for having got rid of almost all of my warm clothing only a few days before. How did I know that it would snow in the middle of June!?! Even in Minnesota, a snowfall in June would be a very rare occurrence. I certainly wasn't planning on winter camping. I felt like burrowing deeper in my sleeping bag and hibernating in my tent for the next 2 weeks—anything to avoid the cold that was now chilling my bones.

I wore everything warm I could find. I wore a long sleeve t-shirt, with a hooded sweatshirt. I had no long pants, so I wore extra underwear under my bike shorts. I wore a baseball cap under my hoody. To protect my exposed legs as much as possible, I wore a pair of wool socks that stretched almost to my knees. I wore my other pair of wool socks along with my bike gloves around my hands. I was basically wearing everything that I had left in my pack, and it was still so cold. I headed to the nearest diner to warm up and contemplate my next move.

I was doing this trip on less than a shoestring budget, so I didn't have the luxury of staying in hotels and waiting out bad weather. Time really was money, and each day I saw my meager funds slowly trickle away. There was no real choice. I had to cover some distance each day—I had miles to go. The news got worse as I was trying to warm up by drinking coffee in the diner. I learned that Yellowstone was closed because of the snow. They were not sure when it would reopen.

It was cold, and the wind was biting, but I knew I had to keep riding and inch my way closer to Yellowstone. The clouds were low and overcast with the temperature hovering around freezing. Periodically, it would spit rain, and in the higher elevations the rain would turn in to sleet. It was an eerie feeling at times, riding above the tree line with snow on the ground and clouds directly in my midst—like I was in some kind of a whiteout. At times, visibility was reduced to less than 50 feet. Coming down from the higher elevations, the sleet would pelt me so hard that I had to wear my sunglasses to help shield my eyes and face from its sting. It felt like hundreds of needles poking me all at once, pummeling my face as I biked on through the cold and worsening conditions. The only way to stay warm at all was to keep biking.

Finally, in the late afternoon, I found a First Baptist church in West Yellowstone that was offering free lodging for travelers caught in the storm. If there was a God in heaven, that God was residing in West Yellowstone. It was definitely a welcome sight, being able to stretch out my sleeping bag on the floor of a heated church. The thought of having to put up my wet tent in the snow sent a shiver up my spine. It was heavenly to be in a place that was dry, where I could thaw out and warm up. And they were offering a free chili dinner to boot!

The next day I became a very good Baptist. They had their service that morning, and I felt obliged to attend, given the generosity of their spirit from the night before. There must have been 30 people in this small country church attending service. At one point, they asked if any of the travelers would like to give a testimonial. I spoke up about how I saw the presence of God in so many ways on this trip, the most recent examples being the angel couple in Idaho and the generosity of this church offering us food and shelter from the cold. I could tell I was winning points from the congregation as a looked out at a sea of nodding heads, seeming to agree with what I was saying. Right after the service, I heard the news that made my day: Yellowstone had opened up for travelers that hour. Soon I was packed, bundled up, and heading out the door, saying my last goodbyes.

The snow was melting, but it wasn't exactly balmy, June weather. I was still freezing as I entered the just-opened Yellowstone National Park.

Yellowstone was the first national park in the United States, established on March 1, 1872 by President Ulysses S. Grant. Yellowstone encompasses 3,468 square miles, larger than the states of Rhode Island or Delaware. It is 63 miles north to south and 54 miles east to west. Lava flows and rocks from volcanic eruptions cover most of the area of Yellowstone. It is home to over 60 different species of mammals, including over 30,000 elk and over 300 grizzlies. It is also home to one of the world's largest petrified forests, and the largest active volcano field in the world. In 2011, they had recorded over 1,000 mini earthquakes in the park.

I was so cold bicycling through Yellowstone that I would stop at every rest stop in the park, spaced about 10 miles apart, get under the hand dryer and punch it about 20 times to warm up my hands and body until feeling came back in to my extremities, only to rush back out and pedal in the cold for the next 10 miles to stop at the next rest area and sit under the hand warmer another 20 minutes before heading out yet again. This was my ritual of survival as I inched my way through Yellowstone. This is what I remember most about Yellowstone, outside of its panoramic beauty.

It was in Yellowstone that I was hit by a vehicle. I was riding on the shoulder of the road, near some elk and buffalo. At times in the park, because of high vehicle density, it was not unusual to see bumper-to-bumper traffic—not the place to be if you are in a hurry. Actually, it is a wonder there are not more accidents in the park, because there is so much to see. That's the problem; you have a bunch of drivers becoming completely distracted behind the wheel, looking at everything but the road ahead. It was not unusual to see tourists hanging out the windows, leaning out taking pictures of bear, buffalo, and sometimes mangy looking bicyclists.

At one point, a large Winnebago I had passed earlier was inching its way up, meandering out of its lane, and onto the shoulder I was on. Good thing it was only going one or two mph faster than me, because the next thing I felt stunned me—its side-view mirror slapped me on my upper back. Luckily, their window was open and I could yell out, "Hey, what are you doing? I'm biking here!" They immediately slowed down, aghast with the sudden realization that they had run into me, and pulled back into their lane.

I would have liked to linger longer in Yellowstone, and explore the Grand Tetons further, but I was too cold. I was able to see Old Faithful, enjoy some of the wildlife, and take in Yellowstone Lake, one of the highest fresh water lakes in the world, at close to 8,000 feet above sea level. Soon I was leaving the park, and heading to Dubois, Wyoming, about 50 or 60 miles east of Yellowstone.

Dubois, Wyoming, has a population of 962 people. Butch Cassidy owned and ran a ranch just outside of town in 1890. This was the only place on my trip where it was so windy, I couldn't put my tent up. Instead, I threw my sleeping bag on the ground and slept next to my bike. The next day, in the town diner where I got breakfast, I found out that the area where I had laid down my sleeping bag for the night was apparently inhabited by rattlesnakes. The thought of one of those snakes squirming in to my warm bag in the middle of the night was enough to give me goose bumps.

Every state featured something memorable on my trip. Oregon featured the ocean and mountains, Montana the snow, and Wyoming featured wind and desolation.

Wyoming became our 44th state in 1890. It is the least populated state in the union. The western two-thirds of the state are mountainous, while the eastern third is high-elevation prairie. Wyoming is where the Great Plains meet the Rockies. Wyoming has the distinction of having elected the first woman to office and being the first state in which women won the right to vote.

The prevailing wind currents in the United States blow from west to east. The general consensus is that if you are going to bicycle across the United States, you should bicycle from west to east to take advantage of the westerly winds. However, the Bikecentennial route through Wyoming had more of a north-to-south direction than east-to-west. Consequently, I found myself bicycling against the wind, or at least a crosswind, for most of the time I was traveling through Wyoming.

After a while, the wind can be demoralizing, especially when you are expecting more of a tailwind and instead you are biking into a strong, unrelenting headwind. The wind would be blowing so strong in my face in Wyoming that at times, bicycling on a flat surface, I would have to gear down to my third, second, or even first gear and pedal at a rate just beyond a walking pace.

In fact, I decided that I would much rather bicycle up steep mountain passes than into the wind. Why? Because you see mountain passes coming in the distance, and you steel yourself for the unrelenting strain of the climb ahead. Eventually, you get to the summit, pedal like hell on the way down, going as fast as you can as a reward for the pain of the previous climb, and then it's over. With the wind, though, you can't see it; you can only feel it. The wind can pound you relentlessly all day. You can spend a whole day bicycling against the wind and it may never let up. After a while, the wind begins to erode your mental and physical stamina, and you begin to wonder, "When the hell is it going to let up or die!?!" No, give me mountain passes any day over the wind!

Wyoming has some of the longest, empty, desolate spaces in the United States. It has a population of 500,000 people and over 2 million sheep. Outside of Alaska, it has the lowest rate of population per mile, at just over five people per square mile. It was not unusual to go almost a whole day of biking and see no one. In fact, at one point (this is when I knew I was beginning to lose it) I was starting to talk to the cows and sheep along the way. I'm a very social person, and when there is no one to talk to, I do the next best thing. During one hot afternoon, I had to go to the bathroom really bad. I decided to defecate in the middle of the road, right down the striped line, to see if I could get away with it. On this particular day, I hadn't seen any cars or signs of wildlife for hours. There I was, my white ass flopping in the wind doing my thing, and not even a crow was around to witness the act—thank God! That would have been quite the scene, if a car suddenly stumbled upon me with my bare ass hanging out in the breeze! That's when you know it is a pretty desolate place, when you can get away with a stunt like that.

One thing I discovered is almost every small town in America has its own Fair Days—out west they were frequently called Rodeo Days. Basically, these events were an excuse for the town to have a big party in the middle of the summer. In the sprawling town of Saratoga, Wyoming (population 700), down in the south-central end of the state, near the Colorado border, I arrived in the middle of their Rodeo Days. There was only one campground, and that was in the middle of the town, which happened to be where the rodeo days were being held. I was too tired to pedal on into Colorado, so I set up my tent among the other couple dozen tents that were already set up.

You could hear the band playing down the block, and the smell of fair food in the air: cotton candy, hot dogs, kettle corn, and of course beer, lots of beer. They had the carnival in town, complete with a Ferris wheel, dunking tanks, and a merry-go-round.

I must have been totally exhausted from biking against the wind all day. I'm usually a very light sleeper. In fact, I'm such a light sleeper that if you winked your eye from across the room, I might wake up. On this particular night, with the sounds of the merry-go-round and the distant band ringing in my ears, I fell asleep soundly, not waking up once in the night. The next morning, when I woke up around 5:30 or 6 a.m., it was very quiet outside my tent. As I broke down my camp and surveyed what had transpired that night, I was reminded of the band, The Who and their song about "Teenage Wasteland."

Strewn around the park in the quiet morning hours were people who had passed out drunk. Some were still holding a bottle and others had unzipped the tent flap, but hadn't quite made it in, spending the night sleeping half in the tent and half out. There were so many people passed out, lying on the ground, that I had to wheel my bike around them as if they were corpses, because I was afraid if I started biking, I might run over an unsuspecting soul. It was like walking through a mine field.

That was my last image of Wyoming as the wind blew me in to Colorado.

# CHAPTER 11

# Love is a Many Splendored Thing!

*Say hey . . . I'll be gone today*
*But I'll be back comin' round the way*
*Seems like everywhere I go, the more I see the less I know*
*But I know one thing, that I love you!*
*I love you, I love you, I love you!*

*"Say Hey"* by Michael Franti and Spearhead

As I biked across the country, I would occasionally see couples bicycling together. Sometimes I would even see them on bicycles built for two, better known as tandems. I always thought, what a great way to see the country together, bicycling on a tandem.

When I embarked on my cross-country bicycle trip in 1981, I was 22 years old and I had never kissed a woman before. I had never made love to a woman nor been in a relationship with a woman. Romance for people with disabilities rarely happens, or if it does, we usually start much later than the average able-bodied person. If disability was considered attractive in this country, then magazine stands would have all kinds of pictures of us gracing their covers, but last time I looked, that wasn't happening.

I could never remember a woman ever being interested in me. No one ever approached me and asked me out. When my brother and I attended St. Scholastica, I had a crush on a fellow classmate named Holly. Holly only had eyes for my brother, and then eventually my roommate, Dan, whom she later married. In my experience, when you have a disability, women look past you. Or if they looked at me, all they saw was my disability and nothing else. Oh, I had many crushes, but they were always secret; no one ever knew. I even went on a few dates, but they were what I call "mercy dates"—women who basically didn't know how to say "No" to my date request, so instead went through the torture of a date with someone (me) they did not want to go out with, and seemingly counted the minutes until they could gracefully depart from my presence. I spent a lot of time alone, and had far too many moments of loneliness in between those mercy dates.

Now, 30 years later, not much has changed. Oh, I've had a few relationships since then, even got married once, but as I write these words, I'm still alone. A couple of years ago, when I was planning another bike trip to Glacier, Banff, and Jasper National Parks, I was alone. But by the time I left for Banff that summer, I had met what I was convinced was "The One." Molly and I had met on the Internet 5 months earlier and by that Christmas, we were engaged. I was "her soul mate," her "last first kiss," as she would always fondly tell me. Then, 8 months later, seemingly out of nowhere, Molly sent me an e-mail breaking off everything, without even a chance to talk on the phone or meet in person. She broke it off "to find herself," much to my sorrow and despair. A soul mate for me apparently had a shelf life of 18 months. So much for happily ever after.

This setback of the heart certainly made me pause; I revisited all my past relationships in an effort to learn more about this whole idea of what love really is. I decided to investigate even further, and set out on developing a course at our college on the whole topic of love.

Amazing. When you Google™ the word *love*, over 4 *million* different webpages are devoted to some aspect of love. Perhaps it says something about our society when so many of them relate to porn. So many of our songs and movies are devoted to some theme or aspect of love. Yet as a therapist, educator, and resident of Planet Earth, I'm convinced that so many of us really know so little about what love is. Like the blind men describing the elephant, we have pieces and hints of what love is all about, but do we ever really hold on and capture the essence of what love is all about, and what it all entails? The study of love in the academic world did not begin to receive much attention from scholars until the 1970s. The main reason for a lack of scholarly investigation was that love was considered to be too elusive of a concept for psychologists to study.

Never in our recorded history has there been so much pressure to find one's soul mate as we have today. Only a little over 100 years ago did we begin to cite love as the major reason for marrying someone. Over the history of civilization, love was not the main reason why people married. People's main incentives for getting married were based much more on economic and survival motives than on love. The ancient Greeks referred to romantic love as the "madness of the gods."

Today, the term *soul mate* is thrown around as commonly as the words *dating* and *marriage*. The Atlanta psychiatrist, Frank Pittman, states, "Nothing has produced more unhappiness than the concept of the soul mate." We expect our *knight in shining armor* or our *princess* to be all things to us. This illusive soul mate is supposed to overlook or make up for all of our own deficiencies of character, to accept us unconditionally, to know exactly what to say in every situation, to be able to read our minds without us having to even speak; to be this incredible lover who triggers uncontrollable orgasms just from his or her scent, our intellectual equal, our dearest friend and confidant. And then we wonder why we get so disappointed in our love relationships when a supposed soul mate turns out to be far less than this template we seem to have imbedded deep within our collective psyches. As I frequently tell students, dating is to marriage as travel brochures are to the actual destination.

I talk with my students all the time about how we are so consumed with preparing for and getting a career. As a little kid, one of the first questions you hear from grown-ups just after you learn to walk and talk is, "What are you going to be when you grow up?"

To love and to be loved, after food, water, and shelter, is one of our most basic needs, desires, and motivators. Yet so many of us are starved for love, and so confused by it. As the author Eric Fromm once said, "People are starved for love; they watch endless movies about love stories, they listen to hundreds of songs about love—yet hardly anyone thinks there is anything to learn about love."

I spent almost 10 years in college completing three different degrees in my preparation in becoming a marriage and family therapist. I took courses on counseling, interpersonal communication, marriage, family, human sexuality, psychology. I read way too many textbooks and research articles in the field, but never was the word *love* mentioned by my professors or any of the authors I read. And yet so many of the clients I saw in therapy had a crisis of the heart—problems centered on love or lack of it, or about confusion around it or even what it means.

The author Leo Buscaglia said in his book, appropriately titled *Love,*

> *We form what we hope to be permanent relationships in love with people who have hardly any knowledge of what love is. They equate love with sex, attraction, need, security, romance, attention, and a thousand similar things. Love is all of these and yet none of these.*

With the proliferation of dating sites and chat rooms, the Internet has become a virtual mega-mall of choice for eligible partners. We have an unprecedented number and variety of potential partners available to us from the comfort of our own homes. You don't need to go to the local singles bar or fitness club. The biggest pickup stage is found on our computers with the proliferation of dating sites: Hispanic singles, Asian singles, Christian singles, spiritual singles, elder Singles, and disability dating sites. Anything you might be looking for you can find with a click of your mouse from your own den. It has become the virtual supermarket of dating with aisles of choices to choose from.

The problem is there may be too much choice. "The grass may be greener on the other side of the fence" seems real in today's online market of potential soul mates. Sure, there may always be someone out there somewhere in cyberspace that may be a better fit, that could be your soul mate. But because there is so much choice, commitment in a relationship may become a more elusive reality than ever. An old Guindon cartoon strip from the *Minneapolis Star & Tribune* in the 1970s showed a woman getting a big diamond engagement ring; she said to the man, "I do for now . . . until someone better comes along." Today, it appears that more and more people in relationships have one foot in and one foot out, with an eye always open for something better out there. Consequently, we put so much pressure on marriages and relationships to fulfill some idealistic, elusive concept that falls far short of being real.

What most people are looking for in a love relationship is true intimacy. But paradoxically, the thing that most frightens us is true intimacy. True intimacy is scary and is really a grown-up skill. Intimacy involves vulnerability, risk—an openness and honesty that most hardly ever visit, but seldom stay in. Intimacy is a movement toward honest self-disclosure, more about being truly known and less about being validated. One exercise of intimacy that I've adopted from *The Psychology of Love* by Nathaniel Branden (2008) is to invite my students who are married or in a long-term, committed relationship to try to spend an uninterrupted 12-hour period with just themselves and their partner. There can be no TV, computer, stereo, or phone in the room. They cannot talk about school, work, kids, or family. They cannot play board games, drink, or sleep during this period. The exclusive topic of conversation must be about themselves and their relationship, that's it.

Usually my students respond to this challenge with either excitement or fear. We are misnamed as "human beings" because we spend most of our waking hours *doing* rather than *being*. Perhaps a more accurate self-descriptor would be "human doings." People may be apprehensive and anxious over the unknown. "We are going to talk to each other, we are going to have to be with each other for 12 hours!?"

Intentionally placing themselves in a situation with no diversions or outside stimulation, they begin to encounter only themselves.

They begin to understand the meaning of intimacy. They begin to peel away layers that lead to greater emotional connectedness and aliveness. They begin to encounter who they are as individuals and as a couple. They inevitably end the day happy. Occasionally, it doesn't end on a happy note; the couple may discover how empty and ill-suited they really are for each other. They may decide to no longer remain together. But I label this, too, as a success in the experiment. The real tragedy would be to stay on together in a loveless, empty relationship where the illusion is that you are together, when in reality, you stand alone.

One key factor that shows up again and again in long-term, successful marriages is the full acceptance of the other. Couples that have been happily married 40 or 50 years are no longer trying to change the other. They just accept the other person for the way he or she is. As a former marriage and family therapist, so often with the couples I worked with, I would see that each of them would be trying to change the other. It never worked.

I'd ask a beleaguered wife, "So how long have you been trying to change him?"

She would respond, "Probably ever since we got married."

"So is it working for you?"

"No, it is totally frustrating." She would look down at the floor in utter defeat and frustration.

"So let me see if I got this right. You continue to do more of what's not working in the hopes it works. Why not work on accepting him just the way he is?" My advice would sound simple enough, but few people ever followed it.

Reflecting back, I'm glad I no longer do marital therapy, because it rarely ever worked. First, most couples would wait until their marriage was terminally ill and on life support before they would drag themselves into therapy as a last resort. Then, after years of bitterness and resentment had built up between them, they would give therapy a try. This usually meant that they came to one or two sessions, gave this therapy thing a couple of hours of their precious time, and because I couldn't do magic and cure their ill begotten relationship in a couple of sessions, they would declare to family and friends later, during their divorce, that "we gave therapy a try, but it just didn't work."

The reason marital therapy usually fails is because most people come into therapy wanting the therapist to "fix" the other person. They are invested in seeing the other as the problem. Rarely do they come to therapy open to the possibility that, for real change to occur in the relationship, each of them needs to step up and take individual responsibility and accountability for why things are as messed up between themselves as they were. The big secret is, if you want to change the other, it always begins with changing yourself first. But most couples coming in to therapy don't want to change. They want the other to change because they think, "There is nothing wrong with me."

The other thing that happened frequently in marital therapy was that each partner wanted me to take his or her side. Usually one, or both, on some level, felt victimized by being in a relationship with the other. Consequently, one of two things happened. Either they grew frustrated and disillusioned because I wouldn't take their side, or one of them would drop out because in some illusionary way that was beyond my scope of understanding, one would inevitably accuse me of taking sides with the other—something you learn never to do in any graduate school training in becoming a marriage and family therapist.

In the human sexuality class that I teach each semester, we spend an entire evening, a 3-hour class, looking at the whole topic of love. I approach the subject with a great deal of humility, knowing full well, like a student myself, that I don't have all the answers, and (to my credit, I hope), I don't pretend to know everything about love. But it is one of the most exciting topics to explore, and certainly one of my most popular subjects in the class, promoting a great deal of discussion and debate.

I begin the class asking them to get together in small groups, and I have them draw a big heart on some flipchart paper at each table. They must begin by answering the question, "What is love?" They soon realize that it is more than a feeling, more than a thought, and more than a decision. Love is all of this and yet none of it. Why? Because to begin to define love is to limit it. Just like the minute you begin to define who God is, you limit God, you compartmentalize and label God. So it is with love. The minute you start to attempt to define love, you limit it, you begin to minimize it. I don't think you can ever really define love, or God.

To get the students a little deeper into their analysis, I ask them,

> So when does it go from *like* to *love*? How do you know? Does your "Head yell down to your heart, 'You better look out below'" (lyrics from an old John Prine song)? Does a neon sign start blinking on your forehead, "You are now entering the love zone"? Does it go from *like* to *love* when you sleep with someone? We discover that so much of what we think is love is really infatuation and dependence. We discover, despite all the songs about love and all the hits on Google™ when you type in the word *love*, we really know so little about love.

Over the years, in looking at this elusive topic called love, my students have concluded that very little of what we call love is un-conditional. Especially in relationships, if you really look at it, most relationships seldom involve unconditional love. Most relationships are very conditional.

I remember my major professor and friend in my marriage and family therapy program, Tony Jurich (former president of the American Association of Marriage and Family Therapy), saying to us how most marital relationships involve multiple contracts on multiple levels, most unspoken, but nevertheless very real. We have the explicit vow or contract of "until death do us part," but most marriages have implicit contracts that reveal a very conditional level of love. The conditional aspects might be stated something like this: "I will stay with you as long as you don't cheat," or, "I will stay with you as long as you don't become a quadriplegic/alcoholic/drug addict," or, "I will stay with you as long as you continue to lavish me in certain socio-economic level." But as soon as any of these expectations vows are broken, one partner is usually running out of the relationship.

So we begin to see that there is really very little of what we call *love* in the world. Most love, we discover, is very conditional, and when love has conditions, judgments go with it. With conditions and judgments, it is no longer love. The only true love is unconditional love, but we discover that is very rare indeed.

Perhaps the authors of the book *Love Is a Mirror* gave us a hint of what love really is all about: "Perhaps love is the process of my leading you gently back to yourself. Not to whom I want you to be but to whom you really are."

At this point in the evening class, my students are fully engaged in the topic. After all, this may be the only time in their life, their academic career, that we examine something we all desire but seldom understand. This is when I give them the following quote by one of my favorite authors, Anthony de Mello. De Mello was a Jesuit priest who grew up in India, ran a retreat center there, and wrote numerous books on spirituality. He died abruptly in 1987 at the age of 57. Some have since then labeled him a modern mystic.

Anthony de Mello said that, "We fall in love with our idea of that person, what we need that person to be. Seldom do we fall in love with who they really are." I have my students ponder and debate this for quite some time. Most end up agreeing with this statement. Seldom do we truly see the truth of anyone. We see what we've been conditioned to see, what we hope to see; but seldom do we see what's really there. Our perceptions are always biased and always partial. So much of what we call love is our hope, our desire for what we think that person is. So much of what we think is love is need-based. Many of us enter our love relationships from a place of diminishment, a place of our own woundedness. No wonder love becomes so elusive, coming from this state of being. So many of us look for love outside of ourselves, when we have yet to find love within ourselves first.

An example of how little we love ourselves is also found each semester in my human sexuality class. I ask students to close their eyes and raise their hands if they can honestly say they love every part of their body. It is striking how often no one raises their hands, or perhaps one or two at best, in response to the question.

In talking about love, Erich Fromm stated that, "Love is an act of will, a resolution to commit my life completely to that of the other person. To love somebody is not just a strong feeling—it is a decision, it is a judgment, and it is a promise. If love were only a feeling, there would be no basis for the promise to love each other forever for a feeling comes and goes."

Near the end of class, I say to my students, "So, do you want to know the secret of life?" By this time they don't know if I'm joking or for real. So I say it again, a little more emphatically: "Do you really want to know the secret of life?" I get more yeses, and then I tease them, "I guess you really don't want to know." Then they come back to me in unison, "YES TOM, WE REALLY WANT TO KNOW; TELL US THE SECRET OF LIFE!!!"

I then say to them, "Well then, lean in. Is everybody leaning in?" Then, in a more quiet and deliberate voice, after everyone has quieted down I say: "It involves one word." Some of them begin to guess and they are always wrong. And then I say, "I know it without a doubt and I'm willing to debate anyone on it. But just think, on this day, you will discover the secret of life. What a bonus for you!! The secret of life is one word. The secret of life is *RELATIONSHIPS*. Yes, the secret of life is relationships."

How do I know that? Early in my career in working at the Cancer Center at St. John's Hospital in Santa Monica, California, I saw a number of my patients die. I was there as they took their last breaths. I was their social worker, and I got to know many of my patients well during their final days. Not one of my patients that died ever said, in facing their imminent death: "Gee, I wish I would have bought that house," or, "I should have bought that boat, or taken that trip." If they shared any regrets at all, it always centered on the theme of relationships: "I wish I had told her I loved her more"; "I should have appreciated him more"; "I should have spent more time with her." What really mattered wasn't about things at all, it was always about people and relationships.

To further prove my point to the students, I mention that there are over 400 theories of counseling in the field of therapy. The research shows that the number one curative variable in working with clients, regardless of the theory in use, is the quality of the relationship that is formed between the client and the therapist. So indeed, I truly believe that the meaning of life revolves around relationships. We gain our greatest meaning, our greatest purpose, through the quality of the relationships in which we involve ourselves. And finally, what we know from successful college graduates is that most people can point to a teacher, professor, or coach who believed in them (again, speaking to the power of relationship), sometime during their educational process, who was integral in helping them become successful in completing their degree.

Love is indeed "a many splendored thing." True love is healing, transformative, for it always leads you back to you.

# Colorful Colorado

*And I've got such a long way to go*
*(Such a long way to go)*
*To make it to the border of Mexico*
*So I'll ride like the wind*
*Ride like the wind.*

By Christopher Cross, *Ride Like the Wind*

Colorado is called the Centennial State because, the 38th state to be admitted to the Union, it became a state in 1876, our country's centennial. Colorado is home to four national parks and it contains the 30 highest peaks in the Rocky Mountains.

Colorado was the only state where I met family along my journey; hit the highest point of the trip; met my future sister-in-law; pedaled my longest 1-day mileage total in the entire trip; and almost got killed.

It was good to be out of the wind of Wyoming, but now I was entering the most mountainous state of the trip. Colorado is home to the southern Rocky Mountains, and the altitude is most daunting. The lowest point in the whole state is still over 3000 feet.

I was still following the route mapped out by Bikecentennial, which took me in a southeastern direction from just east of Steamboat Springs southward to Pueblo; from there, I would go due east into Kansas. At this time in 1981, only 5 years past our country's bicentennial, this was still one of the most popular routes to traverse across the United States on a bike. Consequently, it was not unusual to run in to the occasional bicyclist coming from the east. Usually, we would stop to compare notes. They would tell me what's ahead, and perhaps points of interest to check out and things to avoid, and I would do the same for anyone going west. It was not unusual to hear stories or legends of characters they had passed hundreds of miles ago that I would then run in to a few days down the road. For instance, I heard about a tall Englishman with a long beard who was riding solo across the U.S. with a big Union Jack flag waving off the back of his bike. Sure enough, a few days later, I saw him zipping down a pass with the Union Jack flapping in the breeze, serving almost like a sail, as he pedaled like a mad man into the setting sun.

Another guy I ran into was so exhausted from pedaling in the sweltering heat that he had purchased a 50 pound block of ice, bungee corded it on top of his bike panniers by his back wheel, and periodically hacked off a chunk of ice with his knife and sucked on it as he kept pedaling along.

Just inside of Colorado, I ran into a couple of bicyclists from Germany who were biking from east to west. I remember asking them what they thought of this great country, and they said it was very big and they had never seen so many, as they struggled for the right words, "As you say . . . *house on wheels.*" They didn't know how to describe the many large Winnebagos and RVs they were seeing, so they called them "house on wheels." I called them a lot of other things that were not nearly as complimentary when they would infringe on the little bit of road that was left for me and my bike!

That first night in the Centennial State, I slept in an elementary school in Walden, Colorado with some other bicyclists who were following the same Bikecentennial route. There were about 10 other bicyclists and this would be the only time on the trip that I would share a campsite with so many other people doing the same thing I was doing—biking across the U.S. This was a rare treat, to spend an evening with likeminded people, swapping stories and common experiences from our mutual cross-country adventure. After biking through Colorado, I decided to deviate from the Bikecentennial route, so this ended up being the last time I shared a lodging spot with other cyclists.

That night, I was complaining loudly about eating peanut butter and jelly sandwiches for dinner for what seemed like the 100th time in row, when an older bicyclist told me, "Tom, sometimes you eat for taste and sometimes you eat to fill space. Looks like you're eating to fill space tonight." Because of my limited budget, my dinner each evening would consist of peanut butter and jelly sandwiches. The big thrill was when I would move from chunky peanut butter to smooth or grape jelly to raspberry jelly. I read once in *Bicycling Magazine* that typically, with this kind of cross-country bike trip, the average bicyclist burned around 10-12,000 calories per day. I believe it! Every night I would fall asleep still hungry.

My diet on this trip consisted of eating usually pancakes for breakfast. It was a cheap breakfast and pancakes gave me a full feeling longer than anything else. During the day, I would snack on haphazard things from various gas stations or convenient stores, finishing with peanut butter and jelly sandwiches each evening for dinner. I also bungee corded an empty gallon size orange juice container to the top of my back panniers on my bike, that I would fill with water each day. It was not unusual to refill that gallon container of water a couple times a day. I was so thirsty that it didn't matter to me if the water wasn't cold at all.

Periodically, I would be overcome with tremendous cravings. Sometimes, I would stop in a grocery store and come out eating a whole box of potato chips right in the parking lot, or eat large bags of peanut M&Ms. Sometimes I would buy so much food that I couldn't stuff it in my packs, so I would eat it all right on the spot.

The next night, I camped out at the Green River Reservoir. It was the middle of the week, so there were not many campers in the sites. I was in a particularly remote site, up above the reservoir. What I thought would be a serene, comfortable night of camping, ended up being filled with my own version of trauma.

Some adolescents who had obviously been drinking had rolled into a campsite across the reservoir from me around midnight. They were loud and obnoxious as they began firing bottle rockets at my tent from across the water. Soon I was under siege. What made it more terrifying was when they started shooting their .22 caliber rifle in my direction. (I found one of the bullets by my tent the next morning.) The rifle and teenagers drinking heavily was not a good combination. I surmised, while hugging the floor of my tent, that they were not shooting at me in particular (there is a God in heaven!), but shooting above and around, just for fun. Eventually, they either ran out of ammo or they passed out drunk. Needless to say, I got but a few winks of sleep that night.

As July 4th approached, I ran into more people who would throw lit firecrackers at me and my bike from their cars. Other times, in rural areas, bored adolescents who had too much time on their hands would roll down a car window, slow down with a beer in hand, pretend to offer me a beer, and then, just when I was within striking distance, they would speed up again in a fit of laughter. Little did they realize I didn't like beer, so I wasn't disappointed at all when they sped up and left me in the dust.

Colorado was the one state built for biking with all its paved bicycle paths running through the mountains, and it is home to some major bicycling events, with names like Triple Bypass. As I approached some of the popular ski areas, I encountered more paved bicycle trails. It was a refreshing change of pace to not have to share the road with other motorists, RVs, and semis. It was not unusual to be in the midst mountain passes and run into other bicyclists on training rides. Periodically, they would slow down and ride with me for a mile or two, engage in conversation about my trip, and then speed up to continue their ride and be out of sight in a matter of minutes.

The highest point on the trip, and the last time I crossed the Continental Divide was at Hoosier Pass at 11,542 feet. This was part of the Mosquito Range near the ski areas of Breckenridge, Copper Mountain, and Keystone. It took me about 90 minutes to make it up the 4-mile climb. My legs would quiver from the strain as my bike inched up the pass at a rate of about a fast walk. What was amazing is that by that time, I was now able to bike up the entire pass without having to get off my bike and slowly push my bike over the pass. It felt exhilarating to stop at the top of the pass, drink some water and catch my breath and beam with pride as I surveyed the miles below that I had managed to bike up. All through the state of Oregon, because of lack of hill training, as I approached the top of the pass, I would have to dismount my bike and walk it over the summit. But within the span of three weeks, I had now become strong enough to bike over each pass without having to walk my bike over the summit. For the first time, I finally felt in shape. It took me four states to get to this point, but I now felt invincible. Whatever the trip would throw at me, I felt confident I could handle it.

Up until I reached Pueblo, Colorado, I had averaged 85 miles per day on my bike. My big goal was to someday ride over 100 miles in one day—a *century ride* in the biking world. After riding over Hoosier Pass, I spent the night in Fairplay, Colorado. The next day, I ended up riding the farthest I had ever biked in my life, and completed my first century ride. It was like riding downhill all day with the wind at my back. It was a beautiful, sunny day in Colorado, where the sun shines more than 300 days a year. I was making great time as I picked up Highway 50 by Canon City heading to Pueblo. By noon, I had biked over 80 miles. Not only would I break my 100-mile dream, I would obliterate it. Then, something about as rare as winning the lottery would happen; I ran into my brother. This wasn't something planned or premeditated; this was pure chance, and about as improbable as the Cubs winning the World Series, something they haven't done in more than a century, and counting.

My brother, Bob, was always more than a brother to me. He was my best friend. He was my hero growing up and my confidant as we added decades to our lives as brothers. In 1981, he was running an outdoor program sponsored by the Catholic Archdiocese called C.O.L.S. (Catholic Outdoor Leadership Service) in Denver. It was a summer program for Catholic youth based in Mount of the Holy

Cross, near Leadville, Colorado. This was a wilderness program like Outward Bound, only with a Catholic, spiritual twist. My brother was the director of this program that helped youth learn wilderness skills (e.g., rock climbing, rappelling, and backpacking) in the context of a Catholic, spiritual, leadership orientation. That day he was driving a truck full of supplies up to their base camp at Mount of the Holy Cross, when he looked out his driver's side window and caught sight of something familiar biking in the opposite direction on a bicycle loaded with gear.

"Bro, is that you?" he yelled as he stuck his head out his window as I was whizzing down on the other side of Highway 50.

"Oh my God, is that my Bro?!?!" I said, slamming on my brakes almost skidding into traffic.

By this time he had pulled off the road and had his windows down, smiling in my direction with a look of disbelief. As I crossed four lanes of traffic on this divided highway, I kept saying out loud to him, "I can't believe I'm seeing my Bro! What are the odds?"

It was a wonderful reunion! We kept hugging each other, smiling, and laughing, completely oblivious to the traffic whizzing by. I missed my Bro so much! It was the first and only time I saw any family or friends on the entire trip. There we were, sitting in the cab of his truck, him peeling oranges and giving me juice to drink, and me telling him stories of the journey. As I recall it 3 decades later, the magic of the moment stays with me like the freshness of the dawn. In my 55 years on the planet, this still ranks as one of the greatest memories of my life. To think of the odds of this chance meeting makes me think there was more than just chance at play in this moment.

After an hour of catching up in his truck, we both had to move on. I still needed to bike to Pueblo over 50 miles away, and he was overdue getting his supplies to his base camp. We agreed to meet up in Pueblo at the YWCA, where I would be staying in 2 days.

By the time I left my brother, the storm clouds were beginning to form. In Colorado, they say if you are going to climb a *fourteener* (Colorado has 53 peaks over 14,000 feet), you should summit by noon and then start getting down below the tree line to safety before the afternoon thunderstorms come rolling in. The mountains create their own weather patterns, and Colorado leads the country in deaths by lightning. You can count on storms rolling in as the afternoon wears on, and they come without much warning.

I was pedaling as fast as I could to make it to Pueblo before the brewing storm would spill, but I got nailed by a viscous storm about 15 miles west of Pueblo. The terrain was quite desert-like, and the sky had turned an ominous black. The sky opened up about 3:30 p.m. The wind picked up to 30, 40 mph, with gusts over 50 mph. One gust literally blew me off the road and I wiped out. I had to lean in against the wind to steady myself before I began pedaling again.

I started cursing at the crosswind, taunting it; "Is that all you've got? This is nothing! You ain't got shit!" There was nowhere to take cover and nowhere to hide, or I would have. I was in obvious difficulty with tumbleweeds blowing by and lightning crackling all around me. I remembered an old John Prine lyric (amazing what goes through your mind when you are under duress!): *"Yesterday morning an ill wind came, blew your picture right out of the picture frame. Even blew the candle from underneath the flame, yesterday morning, an ill wind came."*

I was amazed and disappointed that not one vehicle stopped to ask me if I was OK as they sped off, protected and sheltered in their tons of steel and glass on wheels. Luckily, after about an hour, I limped into Pueblo and found the YWCA. I had covered 144 miles that day, the farthest I had ever biked up until that time or since. The whole day was one big downward descent, with the wind mostly at my back. That day I had gone from over 11,000 feet to just above 5,000 feet. Like the Christopher Cross song, I was "riding like the wind" all day long.

Once I had broken the century mark, I regularly topped the 100-mile mark. Of course it helped that I was no longer pedaling in the Rockies. Before Pueblo, I had averaged 85 miles per day. After Pueblo, I averaged 112 miles per day. I broke the century mark 13 times over the next 16 days riding on the trip.

My brother held true to his word and did show up at YWCA 2 days later. At first, I was disappointed that he showed up with his girlfriend, Mary. Initially, I wasn't too excited to have her with us; it was like a third wheel crashing the party. At least she was good looking; she provided a nice distraction. Soon, though, I warmed up to her and could see right away why he was interested in her. They had just begun dating. Little did we realize that 14 months later, Mary would become my sister-in-law.

That night, we shared a pizza and stories that took us deep into the evening before they had to head back to Denver. If anyone in my world could relate somewhat to my experience out on the road it was my brother. Only 4 years earlier, he had paddled down the length of the Mississippi River from Bemidji, Minnesota to New Orleans with two other buddies from his days working as a canoe guide in the Boundary Water Canoe Area in northern Minnesota. Ironically, his paddling trip down *Old Man River*, the Mississippi, took him 52 days to complete. My solo bike trip across the United States going from the west coast to the east coast would take 52 biking days as well (It took 58 days overall but thrown in there were 6 rest days where I did no biking).

Colorado would contain my best memory of the trip, seeing my brother, and also the most disturbing memory.

Once I left Pueblo, the terrain quickly flattened out as I entered the Great Plains of the Midwest. Eastern Colorado may very well have been the most desolate, least populated section of the trip. I was approaching the early part of July, and with each mile I pedaled eastward, the temperature and humidity would rise. By the time I hit Kansas, it was not unusual to see triple-digit temperatures.

It happened in extreme eastern Colorado, on a lightly traveled stretch of highway. My bike was outfitted with a rear-view mirror, so I didn't always have to crane my neck looking backwards trying to see if it was safe enough to move over. I could just look in the rear-view mirror to gauge the traffic coming upon me.

I was pedaling on the shoulder of the road when I saw this large semi-truck in my rear-view mirror, with a silver trailer and a white cab, come around the bend of the two-lane highway. It was in the middle of the afternoon, with the hot sun beating down on my face. What was startling and most frightening was when the truck deliberately pulled over on to the shoulder where I was biking and quickly moved up behind me. Soon his truck was filling my whole mirror, as I wondered in growing disbelief, "Surely this guy is going to move over back on the road!" But he never did. The next thing I knew, I was yelling, "What the fuck!" As my bike careened off the shoulder into the weeds, I leapt to avoid being hit by his truck. After my bike crashed, I looked up from my back side just in time to see him laughing in his side-view mirror as he sped off down the remote highway. I thought to myself, "What kind of a sick human being would get pleasure out of running a poor, defenseless bicyclist off the road?" I cursed at him, shook my fist in his direction, and bicycled off to Kansas.

In that same part of the state, 2 years later (traveling by car), I got caught in a blizzard. I had come to Denver to celebrate Thanksgiving with my brother and his family. I decided to leave early the next day, because a blizzard was blowing in from the Rockies and I wanted to beat the storm. I was playing hide-and-seek with the storm on I-70 across the state. I would get through one section of highway, and they would be closing the road down right behind me. The wind and snow were picking up rapidly with each mile as I motored on in my little, burnt orange Chevette. Finally, maybe 10 miles from the Kansas border, my luck ran out.

Up ahead, it looked like one of those railroad crossing arms that block traffic when a train is coming through. One of those crossing arms was up blocking the whole highway with the State Highway Patrol, and it's flashing lights directing us off the road. They were sending us to a remote town 5 miles down a county road where stranded motorists were supposed to spend the night in an emergency shelter at the local high school.

I told myself, "The hell with that." I'd seen worse storms growing up Minnesota. Besides, I didn't want to spend the night lying on a cold, hard floor with a bunch of strangers who would be snoring all night long. So instead of following everyone else into town, like sheep going to slaughter, I kept going straight on the two-lane country road I found myself on. After all, that was still open. Of course it seemed to go off into nowhere, but nowhere was a better option than sitting around stranded in some no-name town in extreme eastern Colorado waiting for a storm to break and sipping coffee at the local eatery.

I had no map, so I decided to follow my nose. I took any road that was open going in an easterly direction. It didn't matter what size of road it was, as long as it was open; that was good enough for me. Eventually, after a couple of hours of wandering through western Kansas, I stumbled onto the freeway again, and this time it was open. I was proud of myself and my little trooper of a car that we made it home later that night. I didn't think Kansas could look so good!

CHAPTER 13

# Family

*I took it all in childhood*
*But I can't take it no more*
*'cause I caught too much crossfire*
*In your covert war.*

"*Covert War*" by David Wilcox from
the album, "*Home Again*"

When I saw my brother during our short visit in Colorado, he suggested that I call my folks, since they might be a little worried. Until he suggested it, I never thought of calling my folks to update them on my travels. By the time I saw my brother; I had pedaled over 1,500 miles and bicycled through five states during a 5-week period. I decided I would call my folks collect from each new state I pedaled into.

I think about what a contrast that is with my students today. For instance, when my colleague and I organize our annual Katrina trip to the Gulf region, we rent five minivans and hauling five or six students in each van as we drive down from Minnesota to the Gulf over a 2-day period. In the age of the cell phone, it has become almost a fifth appendage with many of our students. It was not unusual in the first couple of years of the trip for our students to be living on their cell phones in the van, invariably with phones either in their hands or in their ears. I would have to put up with overhearing their innocuous calls that would pollute our collective airspace with meaningless conversations that would go something like this:

"Hi, where are you?"

"I'm in Iowa."

"What do you see?"

"Corn fields."

"What are you doing?"

"Oh, I'm at the video store. I can't decide if I should see *Lord of the Rings* for the 12th time or not. Do you think I should rent it?"

"Sure."

"OK."

"I'll talk to you later."

"Bye."

Then, 2 hours later, the people in my van would have to hear their next call, which would go something like this:

"Hi, it's me again. How are you?"

"Good."

"Where are you at now?"

"We're still in Iowa."

"What are you doing?"

"I'm bored, I'm not sure if I'm going to lie out and get a tan or not."

Blah, blah, blah . . . . Enough!!!! I was dying from this stupid drivel polluting our shared air space as we drove towards the Gulf. I resolved it beginning in the second year of the trip, by banning all cell calls while we were in the van. Students would talk to their parents and update them on the most trivial things, like stopping at Wal-Mart for lunch and describing the sandwich they ordered. How did we survive in those primitive days BCP (Before Cell Phones)!

Speaking of survival, I owe my life to a BFGoodrich® tire. Well, actually, it is my dad that owes his life to a BFGoodrich® tire, which ultimately impacted the possibility of my existence as well.

My dad was stationed in Pearl Harbor during the time of the attack on December 7, 1941. He got there by cheating. During his sophomore year at high school in Chicago, instead of taking the final exams at the end of the year, he blew them off and forgot about them until just before he was to graduate his senior year in 1940. One of the priests found him and told him he would not walk at graduation until he passed those long forgotten finals from his sophomore year.

He figured out a cheat sheet, was able to pass the first two exams, and thought he was home free. Then he showed up for the final exam with his cheat sheet securely hidden, when the priest surprised him and said it would be an oral final. My dad's false confidence nose-dived as he bombed miserably and failed the final exam. The priest cut him a deal and said, "Look, you can still walk at graduation, but I'll be at the other end of the stage behind the curtain and you'll have to give me back the diploma until you retake that course." My dad took him up on the deal. Little did the priest realize that he would never see my dad again.

He proudly marched across the stage, received his diploma, and then went out a side door before reaching the other side of the stage. He went directly to the Army Air Corps recruiting office just down the street with diploma in hand and enlisted in the Air Force right on the spot, still in his graduation gown. At the time, he was presented with two choices. He could go to the Philippines or to the Hawaiian Islands. For a 19-year-old, poor, south Chicago kid on the run, there was no choice as his head was flooded with images of girls in hula skirts, the ocean, and the hot sand. He enlisted and was shipped off to the Hawaiian Islands. Years later, he ran into the priest, who accused him of defrauding the government and admonishing him that he should return his diploma, but he never did. Instead, he managed to enroll at DePaul University in Chicago with that diploma.

On the morning of December 7th, after a long night of drinking and carousing that stretched in to the early morning hours in Honolulu, my father was posted on guard duty at Hickman Field. At 7 a.m. on a lazy, Sunday morning, half hung over, he stood watch over a row of fighter planes in a half drowsy state. In the calm morning air of that warm, sunny dawn, he could see in a distance some silver fighter planes in formation diving out of the sky. He didn't think much of it. "Probably some Air Force boys from Wheeler Field having a little fun," he thought to himself. The airplanes were cruising lower and lower, now a lot of them, all headed in his direction. Just then, they started opening up and firing at him. He dove for cover underneath a plane just in time to look up and see these were not U.S. Air Force fighter planes, but the rising red sun of the Japanese Air Force.

Being shot at and diving under a plane for cover did wonders in waking him up and shaking off his hangover from the night before. After the initial shock of comprehending that they were under attack, my father quickly realized that hiding under a wing of a plane propped up next to the plane's tire was probably not the safest place to be. Just then, he heard a loud pop, as a Japanese Zero's bullet was stopped by the tire my father was crouching behind. The plane's tire was made by BFGoodrich®. Over 70 years have passed since that eventful day, but my father has bought nothing but BFGoodrich® tires ever since! (If it was good enough to take a bullet and save his life, he figured it would be good enough to put on any car he was driving.) He then started crawling out to the runway, as far from the row of planes as he could get, as bullets were careening off the tarmac and just whizzing over his head.

At one point that morning, some B17 bombers that were flying in from San Francisco were attempting to land at Hickman Field while the base was under attack. One of the bombers landed within earshot of my father, still crawling across the runway. One of the crew popped out from the fuselage in time to hear my dad yell, "Get down damn it, we're under attack. Get far away from that plane." Just after the crewman said, "OK, Sarge," acknowledging my father's plea, a bullet separated his head from the rest of his body, killing the red-haired man instantly in front of my father.

It is amazing that my father survived the war to become my father. Right after the attack on Pearl Harbor, the feeling was that an invasion of the Hawaiian Islands was eminent. Rising from the carnage of the attack, the military quickly mobilized to set up defenses in preparation for the much anticipated invasion to follow. My father volunteered to go to Molokai in the Hawaiian Islands to help set up defenses out there.

He was waiting on the dock in anticipation of boarding the ship for Molokai when a phone on the dock started ringing. The phone kept ringing incessantly, unanswered. Finally, with great reluctance and impatience, he walked over and answered the phone. The voice on the other end said he needed a half dozen volunteers immediately to stay back and be assigned to another detail. My father volunteered to stay back along with a few others. Shortly afterwards the ship he would have boarded, the Royal T. Frank, was torpedoed in route to Molokai island, killing everyone on board.

After America entered the war, the United States was desperately short of fighter pilots. My father took advantage of a program that was open to enlisted men allowing them to become fighter pilots. Soon afterward, he found himself in flight school. Within 3 weeks of earning his wings, my father was washed out of pilot training for insubordination. With that, he decided to go AWOL, and hitchhiked to his original unit, by then in California, training on B-24 bombers.

Out hitchhiking in the California desert, he was surprised when a limousine pulled up to give him a ride. When he entered the car, he looked up and was blown away to see Bing Crosby shaking his hand and welcoming him in. That night, my father ended up drinking with Bing late into the night, and sleeping over in the servant quarters at Bing's house. From that chance encounter with Bing in the desert of California, my father became an instant Bing Crosby fan and bought every album he ever made.

After Pearl Harbor and being washed out as a fighter pilot for insubordination, my father served in the war in China as a top turret gunner in a B24 Liberator bomber, fighting in the 14th Air Force in China. The much heralded former Flying Tigers now flew fighter support for his squadron. His bomber group, the 308th, had the distinctions of having the highest casualty rate of any bomber group in the war, and also being the most accurate bombing group. They specialized in low-level bombing. Oftentimes, in 1943, they went in unescorted over the target, which contributed to their high casualty rate. The other reason they lost so many crew had nothing to do with the Japanese.

The 14th Air Force was America's smallest Air Force in WWII. They had to fly in all their own supplies from India, over "the hump" (over the Himalayan Mountain range, home of Mt. Everest) into China. According to my dad, they lost more crew to weather over the "hump" than to enemy fire.

My dad's plane was called the "Snowball from Hell" because "they were going to do the impossible and make it through the war without dying." And they did. They survived 63 missions without even a bullet hole in their plane! The most highly defended area in southeast Asia by the Japanese was Haiphong. Bombing missions over Haiphong was where the 14th Air Force lost most of its planes in the war. Both times my father's crew was scheduled to bomb Haiphong, they never made the mission. One time was because of a mechanical problem forcing them to turn back, and the other time because the crew came down with malaria. During his time fighting in China with the 14th Air Force, my father's crew won the Distinguished Flying Cross which is the highest medal you can earn other than the Congressional Medal of Honor.

Six years later, after surviving the war, my father sold all of his meager belongings in Chicago and headed up the Alaska Highway, where he settled in Fairbanks, Alaska, working on the ground crew with Alaska Airlines. It was there that he met my mother, who was an airline stewardess for Alaska Airlines. After eight dates, they were engaged, and married the next year. In 1954, my brother arrived and 19 days after his birth, they moved to Chicago, where my two sisters, Mary and Lilly, were born. I was the "caboose," as my parents were fond of saying, as I arrived in 1958 as the youngest of four children.

I grew up in a very conservative, Catholic family, where God and country went together like pancakes and syrup. My dad flew the flag often; we went to 8 a.m. Mass every Sunday, sitting orderly in the front row. My mother preached that the end of the world would happen, it seemed every year (actually, she still does). I believed that Satan was alive and an active force in the world; that God was a judgmental and jealous God that I needed to ask for mercy and forgiveness on a daily basis; and that the priests and nuns were to be deified and given great respect. They always voted Republican, believed in capital punishment, and thought gays were an abomination to God.

I spent all of my growing up years in suburbia, first living in a sprawling suburb next to Chicago's O'Hare Field called Des Plaines. The planes would come on their final descent right over our house, perhaps a 1,000 to 2,000 feet high. It was so loud when they came over that you had to tell whoever was on the phone at the time to please wait a minute while the plane passed overhead before continuing your conversation. At night, from all the plane traffic during the day, it would smell like an oil field in our backyard.

We moved to Des Plaines on my birthday when I was 4 years old and we lived there until I turned 10 years old, when we moved to Burnsville, Minnesota in 1968. The thing I will always remember about Des Plaines is that it defined the term "urban sprawl." It must have doubled in size in the 6 years we lived there. Multiple blocks of new housing would start up at once. The new homes in various stages of construction provided an incredible playground for playing war or hide and seek. It was always fun when the construction workers would chase us out of homes like a cat chasing a bunch of mice; or in the early evenings or weekends, playing "dodge the cops" that would cruise through the new construction areas. We stepped on many a nail as we scurried out of the forbidden territory, scattering to the winds to evade trouble.

Because of all the new housing, we had dozens of kids moving in to the neighborhood each year, which made pickup baseball games, football games, or any kind of game, easy to start up and play.

My mother was the boss in the family; it was very clear that she was calling the shots and had all the power. She was a devoted Christian who loved her children very much. She was a great believer in the old saying, "Spare the rod; spoil the child." At least once every weekend, one of us was getting spanked for sins of omission or sins of commission. (Growing up Catholic, it didn't matter what it was; there was always a sin to be found). Because each of us was spanked so often, each of us developed our own style of greeting our beating.

(My mother would always say *we would thank her someday for it*. I think she is still waiting for our collective thank you). Ironically, to this day she still carries the "spanking stick" in her car and is very proud of it.

As to our individual styles of "greeting our beatings," my sister Lilly went with pleading: "Please Mom, I beg of you, I will never do it again. Pllllllllllllease don't spank me, I promise I will never do it again." That definitely got the drama vote for creating the most anxiety in the household. This same sister, at 3 years old, had given us a hint of what was to come later. After a particular spanking, she marched down stairs, dropped her pants in front of guests to show her bare bum, and said, "Look what my mommy did. She cracked my popo!"

My brother got the most resentment from all of us. His style of accepting his spanking would be to prostrate himself, and offer himself like a human sacrifice, a martyr, with no resistance, as my mother would hit for distance on his exposed fanny. That style was always thrown in our faces as an example of how to accept your parents' beatings. My sisters and I despised my brother for that; we felt it created such a pathetic example for all of us. The good thing about his style was that it ensured that when my mother wielded her stick to inflict pain, it only hit his most padded area, his butt.

My sister, Mary, and I were what we called in our family "runners." We would run away in terror from my stick-wielding mother, only to be corralled in hot pursuit by our brother and other sister. They would reluctantly corner us, because they knew if they didn't help corral us, they were likely to become a target of my mother's spankings as well. We would not "go gentle into that good night" like my brother, so consequently, in our squirming and twisting, my mother would hit us with her stick regardless of whether it found its mark on a padded area or not (i.e. arms, legs, shins). As I got older, I learned to get up early on Saturday, do my chores, and then leave for the day, to come home only for supper in the hopes that if there were any spankings to be doled out, I wasn't a target.

The highlight of my childhood was our cabin in northern Wisconsin. Actually, it wasn't our cabin; it was my aunt's cabin, named the "Reis Rendezvous" for my mom's and aunt's side of the family. From the time I was 6 years old until I was 11, this was our Shangri-La, escape from the hot, Chicago summers. This was the site of my greatest memories as a child.

It was an idyllic setting for a summer cabin. My aunt got it for a steal from an estate sale that included furnishings right down to dishes, place mats, and bedding. We would get out of school for the year by mid-June and head up to the cabin, about 400 miles north of Chicago, and stay there until a week before school started up again.

Our days would start out by motoring over to Sun Fish Bay in our 14-foot rowboat with a five horsepower motor and play softball at 10 a.m. Mr. Johnson was an old, retired school teacher who had actually built the baseball field, complete with stands, dugouts, foul poles, and scoreboard. He painted everything meticulously in white and red. High above home plate, at the top of the stands, he had also installed an announcer's booth. The game was coed and it included all ages. Sides were picked and each person had a partner on the other team. If you lost the game, then you had to buy your partner a pop in Mr. Johnson's candy shop in back of the stands. The old retired school teacher would organize the teams and then announce the game over the "stadium" intercom system.

It was always fun to get there before the game. We would warm up playing catch out on the field and listen to his favorite polkas ("I don't want her, you can have her, she's too fat for me," etc.) bellowing over the sound system. You could hear the sound of the polkas playing on his record player a half mile away as our boat approached the ball field. I never knew about polka music until I started playing ball at Mr. Johnson's park. The guy was over 80 years old, but he was out there 6 days a week, mowing the lawn, setting the chalk lines, and running the games. Usually on the way home after games, we would try to swamp each other in our fishing boats on the way back to our cabins. If it was nice out, we would spend the afternoon's water skiing and fishing, and if it was stormy out, we would play cards. We used to love going over to our next door neighbor's; she had sons the same ages as my brother and me. We would play cards for hours and our neighbor always had good treats to munch on or would make us great lunches.

At night we would go to the local garbage dump to watch the bears come in searching for food, or play hide and seek in the woods, or sit around a bonfire roasting marshmallows and eating s'mores. We only had the cabin for 5 years, but I will always treasure its memories in my heart.

It was always scary driving up to the cabin. My dad would pile us all in to his 1962 green Rambler, all four kids in the back seat with my mom riding shotgun up front. My dad would ride with one hand on the wheel and the other hand free, ready at a moment's notice to smack any kid who might be out of line. This was not a warm and fuzzy existence.

A couple hours out of Chicago, the freeway gave way to narrow, two-lane highways. My dad was an impatient driver. It was not unusual for him to lose all patience, turn red, and pass a line of 14 cars and trucks on a two-lane highway going about 100 miles per hour, with my mom yelling at him, "What are you doing? Are you nuts?!" while he would be swearing at the traffic. Meanwhile, in the back seat, our eyes would be open wide, filled with panic, as we would see a truck or car coming way too quickly in the oncoming lane, the passing lane we were occupying at the time, only for my dad to swerve back into our lane right before we would die on impact. Each time I thought we were going to die, but each time my father would pull us in seconds before we would meet our maker. I'm sure my brother and sisters and I all have traces of PTSD from the experience! Of course, I probably lost a couple years of my life to the anxiety and trauma in the moment, but hey, we made good time, and I never fell asleep on those trips! Of course when we arrived at the cabin, we would be exhausted from the "near misses" and my mom's voice would always be hoarse by now from all the yelling she did at my dad. Theirs was truly a "match made in hell."

One of the benefits of the cabin was its a refuge from my parents' unhappy marriage. My dad would work during the week and then drive the 400 miles on Friday nights in his little red Volkswagen

Beetle, only to go back to the city on Sunday afternoon. When my Dad was gone, things were much calmer around the cabin; there wasn't that tension that always existed when my parents were together.

My parents were not happily married. The only thing they had in common was four kids and their Catholic faith. The staunch Catholics that they were, they believed in a vow, and divorce was never an option. Instead, they would live in misery their whole lives, hoping that on some level they would win points in heaven. In their later years, they became more like roommates than marriage partners. Today, they don't even share meals together, and when they go to church, they sit in separate pews.

It was no great surprise that I went on to become a marriage and family therapist. Today we would call it "emotional incest." From an early age, I became my mother's therapist. She would confide in me when I was 6, 7, 8 years old, about how unhappy she was with my father. I would come to see my mother as a saint and would be outraged by what my father did or didn't do to my mother. After denigrating him for an hour, she would always add, "But your father is a good man, Tommy." Talk about a double message; what was I to believe, that he was a good man, or the image that she had spent the last hour cultivating, portraying my father as an uncaring, moody, SOB? Unbeknownst to each of us, she was confiding in all her kids the same message about my Dad's flaws.

But that's how I grew up—with double messages, always having to analyze for my own survival the true meaning of each message. Like most therapists, I went into becoming a therapist, on some level, to heal my family and to heal myself. I never did heal them, but I have grown to forgive them and I continue to heal myself in the process.

As the years passed by and I grew in maturity, I could see that there was two sides to every story and I could understand my father a little better. I discovered that my mother wasn't perfect and I grew to appreciate my father and see him through the lenses of compassion and mercy.

We moved to Minnesota when I was 10 years old, in 1968. The moving van was "lost" for two days between Chicago and

Minneapolis. It finally arrived on Thanksgiving Day, the driver now toting a woman he picked up along the way. The driver was unloading the truck until it came time for the refrigerator; when he saw that, he walked off the truck, and instead of turning in toward the house, he kept walking down the road, never to be seen again. That left my brother and sisters and my dad to unload the rest of the truck. That night we went to a local restaurant for our Thanksgiving meal, arriving just as the restaurant ran out of turkey. That was our first Thanksgiving in Minnesota. Welcome to the Land of 10,000 Lakes!

Minnesota was like a new dawn for us. People were friendlier, in general; I never got into another fight. My brother's athletic career soon flourished in high school as he lettered in football, track, and gymnastics. Both of my sisters were involved in cheerleading and their social circles grew. And soon I was to find a lifelong friend.

Rick was the biggest kid in my sixth grade class in elementary school. He and his three brothers had moved there the summer before with their mom and newly married stepdad from South Dakota. I was the smallest kid in the class with the biggest mouth, so it helped that Rick was like my bodyguard. Rick didn't see any of my disabilities; he just saw someone like himself who loved to play sports.

We became frequent visitors to each other's houses. I would load up my sister's "girl bike"(it had no bar in the middle) that was too big for me with my baseball glove, bat, baseball, hockey stick, mask, blocker glove, and hockey net in the baskets over the back wheel where I carried newspapers for my paper route. (That loading up the panniers habit started young!) We would initiate games all over the neighborhood, playing whatever the sport was in season. The hardest ones to recruit were Rick's own brothers. It was an embarrassment to him that his brothers were such whiners! Frequently, we would have to bribe them with candy and pop from the local 7-Eleven® to try to get them to come out and play.

Rick would also spend time at my house. He thought my mom was a saint, and he thought it was cool that my dad was actually around and that he was a war hero (Rick's biological dad spent most of his time in prison, having been arrested 44 times before he died.)

Rick became a friend not just with me, but the whole family. Years later, at my niece's wedding, one of my sisters drew up fake adoption papers and we formally "adopted" him into the family.

Our houses were separated by about a half mile, but in the sports world, it was a great divide. I lived right on the geographic sports boundary, so Rick's teams, no matter what sport, were always winning championships while my teams languished in last place. One year in football, my team didn't even score a point for the entire season!

Rick was a great football player in junior high school. He was our starting middle linebacker on our undefeated junior high football team. His idol was Dick Butkus from the Chicago Bears. The helmet he wore even resembled Dick Butkus' helmet. Football was everything to Rick. Unfortunately, in his sophomore year in high school, he failed his physical; they detected a heart murmur that had never been caught in previous physicals. Rick was devastated.

After his failed physical, we drifted apart. I became more involved in soccer and tennis and he became more involved with partying, girls, and drugs. Even though we inhabited different worlds, we always stayed in touch, and continued to love and respect each other. He continued to visit my mom frequently; she became a surrogate mom/counselor to him, along with many of my brother's and sisters' other friends. My mom was like the neighborhood social worker.

I didn't see much of Rick after I went off to college. He ended up marrying, became a father, got divorced, and lost most of his friends. The idea of "no fault divorce" is a joke. People pick sides and almost everyone chose his ex's side.

Today, over 40 years after meeting in Mr. Spark's sixth grade class, through two countries, living in three time zones, and a couple of divorces, Rick is still my childhood friend and "brother."

My own brother is four and a half years older than me. He was my hero growing up and, like most heroes, I put him on a pedestal until we became adults. He was everything I aspired to be but wasn't—a great athlete, strong, fast, good looking, popular, articulate, charismatic, talented, and a leader. His shadow was large, but I didn't mind being in it; I worshipped him.

My brother was my protector growing up. When older kids picked on me because of my differences, he defended me. He never lost a fight. It is funny how powerful that experience can be; in his presence, I always felt safe and invincible. Years later, when we would go whitewater canoeing (he is a world class paddler) and he would be in the stern and I would be in the bow, we would paddle some hellish class IV rapids—life threatening—but I would always feel safe because I was with my brother, "my protector." I knew all would be well, and it always was.

It was only when we went to college together (he for a second degree) that I discovered that he wasn't perfect. Out of that realization, I saw his "warts" and I took him off of his pedestal. This allowed our relationship to evolve into a more equal, adult-adult, peer relationship, which afforded a greater level of depth and intimacy between us. It was then that he revealed to me that I was always *his* hero. Because of all the barriers and obstacles I had overcome in the person I became, he grew to love and appreciate me even more. It took me a long time to accept that I was actually my brother's hero.

My sisters were always my staunchest supporters and biggest fans. They were as different as night and day. Mary, my oldest sister, was always the "responsible one," the caretaker and the one you could always count on. To this day, Mary is always my "wing-man"; without her, I'm not sure I could have survived all the craziness in my family. Mary and I are probably most alike out of the four of us. My other sister, Lilly, was the easiest for me to be around. I would not see her for months and when we would reconnect, it was like we were in mid-sentence and had never left. Lilly with her ADD, was more distractible and unreliable. But both of my sisters were fiercely loyal to me and would take up my cause with any level of provocation.

Home was never a refuge for me. At 17, when I went off to college, I was never homesick. People on my floor were leaving to go home almost every weekend, but not me. Why would I want to go home and listen to my parents fight and hold such high animosity toward one another? Home was a war zone, not a place of peace, not a warm, welcoming refuge. During my freshman year of college, during which I lived less than 100 miles away, I went home twice, once for Thanksgiving and once for Christmas break.

In my adult years, my parents moved away and eventually retired in the southwest. But the southwest was a place my parents lived in, not a home. I would visit my parents about once a year, more out of obligation than seeking a warm feeling like some Norman Rockwell painting that spoke of the nostalgia of home. Going home was not a fun or easy thing to do; in fact, it was always psychologically draining, and too often left me with a feeling of emptiness.

Now that my parents are in their elderly years (my dad is in his 90s and my mom is in her 80s) and quite frail, going home involves much more work than ever before, as the light of their existence flickers towards extinguishing. Of course, they don't make it easy for any of their children to look in on them when each of us lives hundreds of miles away. For instance, they don't have a computer, a cell phone, or an answering machine. Visiting them is like a field trip into the 1970s. I've pretty much given up calling home, because the phone rings and rings but no one ever picks up because neither of them can hear it ringing.

During one of my mother's latest mini-strokes, eight paramedics and an ambulance showed up at the house to whisk her away to the hospital, and my father, tucked away in his room, never knew what happened because he didn't hear any of the commotion in the house going on right outside his door.

During my last visit home this summer, after repeating myself over and over to my father, and having to scream at him before he could actually hear me, I decided I'd had enough. So I asked him,

"Dad, what's up with your hearing? Why don't you get a hearing aid?"

"Hearing aids are too cumbersome," he replied.

"But Dad, this isn't rocket science; the technology has changed a lot over the years. Hearing aids are really quite advanced now. Besides, doesn't it bother you that you lose so much of the conversations around you?"

"Nope, not really. I'm not bothered at all."

Wow, so much for helping my dad increase the quality of his life. He doesn't want to hear; end of discussion. Of course, there is nothing like being in the car with two people who can't hear. Their hearing impairments only allow them to pick up parts of conversations. So as a rule, every conversation is disjointed. For instance, during my last visit home, on the way to the lawyer's office to update their will, I threw out the statement, "The Minnesota Twins are sure having a lousy season in baseball." My father replied, "Who's having twins?" and my mother said, "I think fall is my favorite season." Ok, so that went over well. On to the next topic.

Usually, shortly after making the pilgrimage to see my folks, my father would send out the "review" in his typewritten letters, which he fondly (and quite ironically) called "short blasts." They truly were "blasts," highlighting what we said or did (or failed to say or do) that usually hurt our mother in some capacity. Over the years, we sarcastically labeled my father's "reviews" as "Epistles of Shame." It is a wonder we ever visited at all, given the consistent reviews of disappointment we would inevitably receive later. Of course, it never occurred to them that what they said or did to my brother and sisters and me would hurt us in any way; it was just a one way street, their children always hurting them.

After years of receiving "Epistles of Shame" from my father, we relabeled going home as visiting *the heart of darkness* (again with a nod to Joseph Conrad). After one particularly shameful review by my father, I created the "Rules of Engagement in Visiting the Heart of Darkness," for my brother and sisters and me to abide by on any visit home. They read like this:

1. Never go home alone. (It was always good to go in with a "wing-man" to debrief the carnage of each day's visit.)

2. Go to bed early, get up late, and take lots of naps. (Going home was like checking in to a war zone. The less you were exposed to "enemy fire," the greater chance you had of getting out alive.)

3.  Always be the visiting team; avoid hosting or being the "home team." (If you were the visiting team you could always escape with errands that you needed to run for your parents, or escape with a sibling for margaritas at the local bar. As a host, I found I had to put so much more effort into entertaining my parents, which was always more draining, since they could barely stand being in the same zip code together let alone the same room.)

4.  Always end the day with a time for debriefing with a brother or sister or friend/spouse. (It was like visiting a psych ward, so to maintain sanity and equilibrium, it was very helpful to debrief and validate that one wasn't indeed going crazy.)

5.  Keep visits short, 3 days or less. (Respect the Mom Maxim we heard growing up: "Company is like fish. Both begin to stink after 3 days.")

6.  Go to church on your own if possible (remembering that my parents are devout Catholics, preferably after a drink or two or three on Saturday night, to avoid having to attend mass at the butt crack of dawn with the folks. I liked my brother's corollary around this even better: Only go to church long enough on Saturday night to get the bulletin, so you could say, "I went to church," to the folks and then go have something to drink to decompress in order to avoid the Pre-Vatican II service. I could swear I heard the mass in Latin once or twice while visiting, or maybe it was the alcohol!!!).

7.  Go for long walks often, or work out regularly—three, four, five times a day, whatever is needed. (Come to think of it, it would have worked better if I would have said, "I'm training for triathlons," more often when visiting, even if I wasn't running a triathlon.)

8. Never talk politics or religion with the folks! (Often I wondered, no prayed, that I was adopted after discussions with my folks around these topics). Even if we never talked about politics or religion while home, I still wished I was adopted. It was depressing knowing that whichever way I voted on an issue, my folks would cancel out my vote by voting the opposite of me.

9. Be vague and skip over details of your life. (This way you become less of a target and invite less uninvited micromanaging by your mother over the course of your life.)

10. Never be caught in any room in the house, the yard, car, or the universe alone with Mom. (Why, you may ask? Because with my mother, it is never a discussion, it always becomes her leading a monologue about herself. You can count on having my mother regale you with stories you began hearing at 4 years old that she repeats hundreds of times over and over again for the rest of your life. In every story, she is the star, and there is a lesson to be learned for your life. If you do, say gently, "Ah, Mom, I've heard that story before." Meanwhile, you're yelling to yourself inside: "I've heard this fuckin' story a million times, and I never want to hear it again!!!" She will, (1) continue on with her story as if your comment disappeared in a black hole, never registering in her psyche; or (2) two, she will shut down in hurt, dripping in guilt directed at you, making you feel in no time like a calloused, ungrateful SOB, leaving you wondering, "Why did I ever bring that up in the first place?" So instead, you eat the pain, go to a beach in the Bahamas inside in your mind, and periodically check in to her story so that you don't miss any key punch lines that may give her clues that you were not listening at all.)

11. Expect written reviews on your visit (see above "Epistles of Shame"). (Always remember that, with each visit, there are

sins of omission or sins of commission, but that either way, you've sinned!)

12. Never ever let our parents see this list. May God be with us all!

As you can see, my family has many flaws and is far from perfect. We have our own issues with each other that seem ever-present. But this is the hand that has been dealt. We chose each other on some level in this incarnation, and they continue to be some of my biggest fans and my greatest teachers, as they show me how and how not to be. As I'm fond of saying to my students in the Family Functions class I teach, "So, if you think you're so enlightened, spend a week with your family and see just how enlightened you really are."

CHAPTER 14

# Wandering

*I've been wanderin' early and late, from New York City
to the Golden Gate and it don't look like, I'll ever stop
my wanderin'. No, it don't look like I'll ever stop my
wanderin'.*

By James Taylor, *"Wandering"*

The state of Kansas was named after the Native American tribe
"Kansa," which means, the "people of the wind." Kansas has more
tornadoes than almost any other state. For thousands of years, it was
settled by numerous and diverse Native American tribes. It became
a part of the United States with the Louisiana Purchase of 1803, but
it did not begin to get settled by whites until the 1830s. In the 1850s,
it was known as "Bleeding Kansas" because of numerous outbreaks of
violence that occurred between abolitionists from New England and
pro-slavery groups moving in from neighboring Missouri. Kansas
became an anti-slavery state in 1861.

Kansas is often thought to be flat. Upon further review, this
notion has been found to be not very accurate. Kansas actually starts
at 684 feet above sea level at the Missouri border and continually rises
to over 4000 feet above sea level by the time you get to the Colorado
border. Recently scientists have ranked it between the 20th and 30th
flattest state in the union.

I have to be the only person in the world that has bicycled across the state and also run in a relay from the state's northern border with Nebraska to its southern border adjoining Arkansas. Little did I realize that within 2 years of bicycling through Kansas, I would end up attending graduate school at Kansas State University. While I was at KSU, living in graduate student housing at Edwards Hall, I ended up running in a relay across the state. Our residence hall director, an avid long-distance runner, came up with a novel idea of running a relay across the state. I was part of a group of runners who lived in the dorm that were convinced by our director in joining the relay.

Our director had an old, beat-up pickup truck with a topper. He recruited seven runners. He outfitted the back of the truck with food and water and a sleeping area. One early Saturday morning in late September, we headed up to the Nebraska border, which was only 70 miles from our campus, and began our great relay adventure. Each person would run a 5-mile shift, and then rotate through so that by the time we reached the southern border at Arkansas, each runner would have run a total of 30 miles in a 24-hour period. We even gained some notoriety by appearing in a very small article (about two paragraphs) in *Runner's World*.

As I pedaled eastward, I reached Kansas at the end of June, and the temperature rose along with the humidity. Eastern Colorado was incredibly dry and desolate. Western Kansas was very flat but much greener, with manicured rows of crops growing as far as the eye could see.

I abandoned my Bikecentennial maps and guide books when I reached Kansas. Too often, the guidebooks would indicate a great place to eat or site to see, only for the place to be closed down or no longer in existence. Bikecentennial provided me a meandering, windy route across the West, crossing the Continental Divide nine times. When I saw the same meandering, windy route for Kansas, I said enough. Kansas has its own subtle beauty, but there was no way I wanted to bike all over Kansas looking for obscure tourist attractions that might not even be there anymore.

Another factor weighing heavily on my mind in Kansas was money. I had no credit cards and only travelers' checks. Despite living an austere existence on the road, my funds were rapidly dwindling away. In addition, by this time, the heat was crawling into triple digits which actually created a greasy, liquid-tar-like phenomenon on the road, making it sticky. It was becoming so hot in Kansas that I gave some consideration to riding my bike at night to take advantage of the cooler temperatures. I decided against this for obvious safety reasons.

The combination of low funds and unbearable heat made me find the most direct route through Kansas I could find. By now, well into the plains of the Midwest, I was clicking off century rides almost every day.

Thoughts of quitting still haunted me daily, with Minnesota only 500 miles away. Home was less than a week's biking away. It was tempting to think of pointing my bike northward. The thought of quitting was like the constant, annoying buzz of a mosquito near my ear. But I would not quit; I couldn't say no to my dream, not after coming all this way. In these moments of self-doubt, I wished that I was biking with others rather than alone. When I would be dragging, or my spirit would falter, it would have been nice to hear words of encouragement, something to lighten the mood or crack a joke. But there was no one there; to get through these moments, I had no other choice but to dig deep within myself. I think I pedaled on because I was too afraid to quit.

By the time I reached Kansas, I had been on the road around 35 days. The ocean seemed far away as I pedaled through waves of wheat, one field after another, with no end in sight, the wind constantly buffeting me one way or the other.

My mental state was becoming more demented. One day it was so bad, I had to crawl into the sauna of my tent and zip up the bug screen to find a refuge from all the flies hounding me as I ate my dinner. For entertainment value, I spread the peanut butter and jelly on my bread and held it to the screen as the flies clamored on the other side, turning the color of my screen to black, as they desperately sought to land on my dinner. I ate with great comfort, taunting them, and knowing they couldn't reach me or my meal on the other side of the screen. I know, pretty deranged alright, but it provided cheap entertainment and I savored in the moment.

In Hutchinson, Kansas, which is almost half way across the state, I met another "angel of mercy." I had been riding about 20 miles when I pulled into a Perkins® parking lot to get breakfast. A nurse, just coming off her night shift at the local rest home, was getting out of her car when she noticed me locking up my bike. Margaret looked to be in her late 40s, about the age of my mom, still in her uniform with an unbuttoned white sweater as she approached me.

"Well you look like you are on some kind of an adventure," she said as she greeted me with a smile.

"Yea, I'm biking across the country," I replied, and I took off my bike gloves.

"I'm going in for some breakfast. Would you like to join me? I'll buy." I couldn't resist a free meal, so I spent the next hour sharing breakfast with Margaret. It turns out she had a son about my age, her only son, who was on a bike trip the summer before when he was tragically killed, struck down by a semi-truck driver in Arizona. I'm sure she saw a little bit of her son in me. I asked her more about her son, and her eyes brightened and sparkled. Her face became more animated as she regaled me with stories about Michael. Some tears trickled down the sides of her cheeks as she shared how much she missed him. She pulled out a crinkled, color picture of her son proudly standing by his bike. I commented on what a good looking young man he was and how I could see some of her in his features.

Soon it was time to depart, and she implored me to be cautious: "Do be careful, Tom, especially with these big semi-trucks passing by. And be sure to stay in touch with your parents and let them know where you are." We hugged and said our goodbyes.

A few nights later, I think I experienced karmic payback for taunting all those flies. I pulled into a campground later than usual.

It was novel to see groves of trees after biking through eastern Colorado and western Kansas and seeing very few trees at all. I was so consumed with getting my tent put up and my dinner prepared that I took no notice of the train tracks camouflaged by the trees. I fell asleep that night only to be awakened by a distant train whistle. After a few minutes I was awakened again, only this time the ground had a slight tremble. I opened my eyes and thought, "Wait a minute, I'm in Kansas, this can't be an earthquake. Why is the ground shaking?" Just then, the train whistle blared and I could begin to hear the swaying and rhythmic rocking of the rail cars on a track. It kept getting louder and louder. Soon, the sound was deafening, and I thought the train was going to go right through my tent. I couldn't stand it any longer, so I ripped open the fly of my tent and looked into the night as the train roared by only 25 yards from my tent. Of course, it must have had over 200 cars, because it kept rolling on and on with no apparent end in sight. Finally, it passed through as I lay on my back, eyes wide open, staring at the roof of my tent. So much for a nice restful sleep! I didn't get a wink of sleep for the rest of the night. Karma is a bitch!

By the end of Kansas, July 4th had arrived. I celebrated by staying in my last motel on the trip. Because of the teenagers-throwing-firecrackers incidents leading up to the 4th, I thought there would be a lot of crazies around for that night, and especially on the weekend, so I got off the road early. That evening I had my brush with fame. When my brother and two buddies had paddled down the length of the Mississippi River from north of Bemidji, Minnesota on foldboats (think wide kayaks), they were interviewed periodically by reporters and were local celebrities in various small communities along the Mississippi as they wound their way down to New Orleans. I, on the other hand, was no celebrity.

In Pittsburg, Kansas, however, a local NBC news affiliate needed filler for a commercial fade-out during their news broadcast. I was it. Before I started on my cross-country trip, friends of mine made a long sleeved t-shirt that said on the back, "Fly coast to coast!" with a picture of a big seagull soaring with wings outstretched on the front. The news people apparently liked the "Fly coast to coast!" in reference to my bicycling across the country. They had no idea that "The Fly" was my nickname in college. In college, my roommates went so far as to make up black t-shirts with yellow lettering that said, "The Fly Fan Club." They made me my own separate shirt that was yellow with black lettering that said "The Fly" on the back. "The Fly" was so popular that at one point I even developed my own line dance, which we debuted in some of the college dances we had that year. For NBC in Pittsburg, Kansas, reporters didn't want to hear any of that; they filmed me silently riding by on my bike, zeroing in my "Fly coast to coast" shirt.

Off camera, they asked me what I thought of their fine state. I felt like saying, after all the heat, the nasty biting black flies, and the kids throwing firecrackers at me as they drove by in their cars, that they could take their state and shove it south of Mexico for all I cared. But instead, I showed great restraint and said, "You have a much more beautiful state than people give it credit for." They smiled and were happy, and I smiled too as I headed in to Missouri thinking I'd never be back in this state again, of course not realizing that I'd be back a year later to start grad school.

When I entered graduate school at Kansas State the next fall, I was nervous. Of course it helped my nervousness tremendously when my roommate, Bill, who had just completed a master's degree at Penn State University the year before, told me not to take school too seriously, as the first thing he unpacked from his suitcase was a nerf basketball hoop which he put on the backside of the door. Bill's whole ensemble consisted of t-shirts and jeans; I don't think he owned one button-down shirt. Last I heard, he was a professor of agronomy at Purdue University.

On my first day, I had to go meet with my major professor, Dr. Anthony Jurich. I had visions of a 50-year-old in a suit and tie, perhaps smoking a pipe. Instead, I was greeted by this guy in his mid-30s from New York City, with a big belt buckle and jeans, wearing cowboy boots, sporting a goatee, moustache, and a black t-shirt, saying, "Hi, I'm Tony. Please don't call me Dr. Jurich. Welcome to

157

Kansas State!" I was blown away! Tony became my big brother, uncle, and academic father all in one. He was larger than life, and he was not only my mentor, but my lifelong friend.

Tony was an abused kid from Brooklyn, NY. He lived many lifetimes in one life. By the time he died tragically, drowning in Mexico in October of 2010 at the age of 63, he had over 500 publications to his name. As a kid growing up in Brooklyn, he had become a heroin addict by the time he was 16 years old. By the time he turned 18, he played lead guitar for the group "Slippery When Wet" that opened for Jimi Hendrix at Madison Square Garden. When he entered college at Fordham University, he played split end on the football team for 4 years. He earned his PhD by the time he was 24 years old at Penn State, and was teaching graduate students at Kansas State by the time he was 25. In his second year of teaching at Kansas State, he won Teacher of the Year. By his 40s, he became the President of the international licensing body of the American Association of Marriage and Family Therapy. He was internationally known and a leader in the field, and yet I, an unremarkable graduate student, mattered to him.

Fifteen years later, on my "Grapes of Wrath Tour," after I lost my marriage and my boys, I came though Kansas, limping in my sorrow, bowed in my depression on my way to my sister's place in Louisville. I stopped to see Tony at his insistence. We had dinner that night and I poured my sorrow on to his plate. He and his wife, Olivia, insisted that I stay overnight with them at their place. The next day, Tony was to spend the day meeting with three professors from Michigan State University, consulting on a project. Instead, he pushed all his meetings back until the afternoon so he could spend more time talking with me and counseling me through my sorrow and pain. I would never forget his incredible kindness.

So one can only imagine the surprise and sorrow I felt when I found out that Tony had died unexpectedly and quite tragically on a beach in Mexico. That morning, Olivia and Tony were walking hand in hand on their favorite beach. Quite suddenly and without warning, a rogue wave crashed in on them, pulling them both out to sea in a gripping undertow. Olivia woke up on the beach coughing and spitting up sand and water, having just been resuscitated before being whisked away to the local hospital. It was unfortunately too late for Tony; he died on the beach.

Months later, Olivia mentioned to me, "I see you every day, Tom. Out of all the thousands of students that Tony had, you were the only one that we ever had your picture on the refrigerator. He thought the world of you Tom, and loved you dearly." I remember hearing that and being stunned. I was just an average graduate student. He had thousands of students; many went on to become reputable professors in the field, with multiple publications, and most earned PhDs. I wasn't a star therapist, but for some reason I stood out to Tony. So much of what I do as a professor and a therapist has Tony's handprints all over it. He will forever be in my academic DNA and in my heart.

By the time I reached Missouri, my funds were dangerously low. I started looking for places to camp out for free. One night, I slept in a 24-hour laundry facility; another night, I stayed at a Salvation Army. I had to go through their religious service, which seemed like a small price for admission to get a free meal, and a cot to boot. I was getting ready to settle in when I discovered my bunk mate was a convicted felon on his way to the Illinois State Penitentiary for violating a probation agreement.

I had never been around a convicted felon before. John was 6' 1" and about 200 pounds. He was my age, but from a different planet. He wore a faded baseball cap, and was built with a v-shaped back. Some would call it a "swimmer's build." It looked as if he had done some serious weightlifting in the not too distant past. He appeared menacing. He was headed back to Illinois because he had assaulted the guy his girlfriend was in bed with.

That night my stereotypes and prejudices about convicts were blown away. We stayed up talking most of the night. He was so fascinating to listen to as he told me all about his life behind bars. At 21 years old, he had already done over 2 years of prison time for assault and battery. He went on to describe the brutality of prison and how, if I ever did time, I would become a likely target for rape and assault because of the weakness of my perceived disability. The next morning, I thanked John for the good company and wished him the best. I pedaled on, crossing both the Mississippi and the Ohio Rivers, as I entered the Blue Grass State of Kentucky.

Periodically throughout the trip, I would be chased by rogue mongrel dogs that would want me for their next meal. Being attacked by foaming-at-the-mouth dogs certainly broke the monotony. The threat of danger quickened my pace as well as my pulse; I would flip into higher gears and pedal like a mad man in an effort to avoid becoming the dog's lunch. After a while, it became a game between me and the dogs. I took some comfort in knowing that if all else failed, I had one of those dog spray canisters that letter carriers take with them to protect themselves while delivering the mail. I never had to use it, until one day riding in Missouri just west of Springfield.

One morning, around 8 a.m., I was pedaling on a quiet two-lane country road. Usually, a dog about to chase me would give me the early warning of a bark or two, letting me know: Game on. But in this case, a larger-than-life coon dog let out no yelp in its sneak attack from the rear. I had no idea it was in full pursuit of me until I felt it breeze by me as it launched itself over me and my moving bike. It came so close that some of its saliva spilled on my shorts. My immediate response was, "Holy shit, what was that?" It quickly turned around and was poised to make another attack.

It looked like a combination of a Rottweiler and Doberman, not the kind of dog I wanted to snuggle up to and pet! Fear gripped me as I realized I had no chance to outdistance this four-legged monster. That's when I reached for the dog spray, hoping like heck that this stuff would actually work. I tested it out by spraying the ground ahead of me; it worked!!! I yelled out, "There is a God in heaven," as I braced myself for the oncoming assault with the mad dog from hell. But an amazing thing happened; the dog ran over to the spot I had just sprayed, took a sniff, and then walked away, wanting no part of me. It must have had some incredibly noxious chemical in it that only dogs could sense (I smelled nothing from the spray) that caused him to back away. Now that I had my "magic spray," I felt bold and empowered. I was stopped and off my bike and yelled in the direction of the retreating dog, "Hey, what's a matter, Chicken? Is that all you've got? You are nothing! You think you're so tough; what a wus!"

For the rest of the trip, when mongrel dogs from hell would come out to "greet me," I would just spray the ground and watch them sniff it and then walk away with their tails between their legs. I took great comfort in knowing this little canister of spray that could fit in my palm was all I would need to protect me from harm, or at least the harm that came from four-legged furry creatures.

# CHAPTER 15

# Love Class

From my human sexuality class, I came up with the idea of a class on love. Each semester when I teach the sexuality class, I cover a unit on the topic of love. In their evaluations, the students usually ranked very high my love unit. I began thinking more seriously about the possibility of creating a course on love a couple of years ago.

Actually, the seed for the love course was planted long ago, in my undergraduate days in the late 1970s. That's when I was first exposed to the "Love Doctor," Leo Buscaglia. He was a professor of education at the University of Southern California at the time. He had started a course on love at USC in the early '70s, and subsequently wrote a book about his experiences in that course, appropriately titled, *Love*. Not long after I read his book on love, he came to my undergraduate college, the College of St. Scholastica in Duluth, where he gave a presentation on his experiences around the topic of love. I was surprised and honored the next day when he showed up at my philosophy class with 20 students and followed up more on his presentation from the night before. From that experience, I ended up reading everything he wrote about the topic of love. I was hooked on Leo Buscaglia's work and ideas.

To the credit of my current employer, Inver Hills Community College, I was allowed to study the topic of love for my 4-month sabbatical. At the end, I had to appear in front of our academic council to convince them that a course on love would be a worthwhile addition to our curriculum at the college. Going to academic council reminds me of seeing the wizard in *The Wizard of Oz*; before you actually see the little wizard, it can be quite intimidating.

When I walked into the council meeting in the board room, there was a long table crowded with various deans, an academic vice president, and numerous faculty representatives sitting at the table. The atmosphere was hot and stuffy—or perhaps that was my own anxiety. The group looked tired and haggard after over 3 hours of listening and debating various course and curriculum proposals. Evidently, the person who presented before me, from the English department, had met stiff resistance, as his proposal was chewed up and spit back out at him with a resounding rejection. As I sat in my chair at the head of the table, easing into face my apparent inquisition, a faculty member kidded with me under his breath saying, "Don't worry, Tom, we cleaned up all the blood, and it should be good now." I wondered how much was kidding and how much was the truth.

As I looked out over my audience, a sea of suits all gazing at me, I could see the skepticism in their eyes and felt like fresh road kill as ravens quickly gathered, circling above me, and waiting for their chance to pounce on me. Their arms were crossed defiantly in front of their chests; some were yawning, rubbing their eyes, and still others squinted at me with disbelief. I paused and drew a heavy sigh, wondering to myself, "How the hell am I going to reach these people? How am I going to convince these people that we need to add a course on love in our curriculum?" Then, from somewhere beyond my imagination, a stroke of inspiration came to me and I went with it. I figured, "What the heck, what do I have to lose?"

I asked them, "How many of you currently have or have had children who are adolescents?" Over half of them slowly raised their hands, each looking around, I'm sure wondering, "So what does this have to do with a course on love?" I then said, "How many of you, when your kids reached 16 years old, did you just throw them the keys to your car and say, 'Alright, here you go. It's time for you to go out driving, since you're old enough. Good luck. I hope you don't kill anybody or injure yourself." I asked, "Did anybody do that with your kids?" They all laughed at the absurdity of it all and concluded unanimously that this would be a stupid idea. They looked a little more alert now. Some even sat up in their chairs, and I paused.

Then I said, "That would be totally absurd, and more than dangerous and unethical, to allow our kids to drive the family car before they passed a driver's education course. Yet we do essentially that with our adolescent children around the idea of love all the time. They go into the world of dating looking for that special guy or girl, and we wish them luck, usually providing little guidance on what true love is really all about (because most of us are in the dark and don't really know ourselves) or what to really look for. And we hope, in all our wisdom, that their fragile hearts won't be trampled on or broken too many times, that they won't grow cynical and hardened. We all hope that they end their quest finding that magical soul mate we've all read about and hoped for and that once found, they can maintain that love bond until 'death do us part.' Of course they go into this with practically zero training. I mean, how many courses on love have you seen?" With such little training, we still expect (hope) they will find that magical someone to spend the rest of their life with.

Where I've taught before, I've seen courses on wine tasting, gardening, karate—but in the six different colleges at which I've taught, in two countries and three states, I've never seen a course on love. We know that, in looking at meaning in people's lives, we know the number one factor in creating that meaning is the number of quality, loving relationships that surround us. Yet we know so little about how to create and maintain these loving relationships, and so often we fail miserably at them."

"We also know that the disciplines of psychology, philosophy, and sociology have always shied away from study of the topic of love. The topic has been seen as too touchy-feely, hard to measure, and not lending itself to rigorous analysis. Consequently in my own research, I discovered there are very few courses on love in college curricula across the United States. When I did stumble upon a course related to love, it was usually focusing on "Love and Poetry" or "Love in Literature." There were no courses that took a comprehensive, holistic view of the topic of love (i.e., the philosophical, psychological, anthropological, sociological, etc. examination of love). Finally, do you know one of the fastest growing courses in college curricula across the US? Go ahead, take a guess. One of the fastest growing courses is the Psychology of Hate. If we have such a fascination for hate, just maybe there's a space and a place to begin to study love."

"I'm thinking, if we were so well taught about the subject of love, I don't think we'd see nearly the amount of divorces and infidelities we see today. Nor do I think we would have so many young people, 20, 21, 22 years old, who are already so lonely, jaded, cynical, and bitter about love and what it means and doesn't mean."

At the end of my diatribe, I looked around the table and, to my great surprise, people were no longer half falling asleep or staring at me with skepticism. They were leaning in, and half way congenial, even cracking a joke or two with me. To my great joy, they had bought my sales pitch. They were going to let me teach the course on love. Of course they had to correct something in giving their stamp of approval, so they made me change the name of the course from "Love Class" to "The Journey of Love and Relationships." Frankly, I didn't care what they named it, as long as I could now teach the course.

Spring semester finally came. With much anticipation, I walked into my first Love class. The classroom was packed. I had approved a two- or three-student overload, so the classroom was filled to overflowing. I had a sense that I was on to something. None of my other classes was this full. It was the great unknown for me, never having taught the course. Just like the students, I didn't know quite what to expect. I did know there must be a million songs and poems on love, so each week students would take turns and we would start each class with a poem that a student either wrote or found pertaining to some aspect of love. Then another student would play a song on love, and say why he or she chose the song and how it related to the course. I half stumbled upon this nice way that worked well to set the stage for each class.

After about the third or fourth week, I found myself doing something at a night class I had never done before; I was hanging out with students 15 minutes, a half hour, and sometimes over an hour after class was over, informally talking about what transpired in class. Usually in my 22 years of teaching college, after a night class, everyone scatters quickly in a race to get back home. Then I received an email from a student, pointing out to me how many students stay after class discussing aspects of the Love course in the hallways and parking lot. Something amazing was happening to my students. They couldn't get enough of the class. About 5 weeks into the semester, we were supposed to miss a week of class due to Student Success Day; a day of classes is canceled and students spend the day on campus going to various workshops and keynote addresses to help motivate and guide them in becoming better students. But the students voted to have the Love class anyway on our usual Tuesday night. So I held the class and only two students missed it.

My syllabus served as a vague guide to the territory ahead; it certainly didn't operate as a strait jacket. About a quarter of the way into the semester, I discovered a giant omission to the course; I had no unit on self-love. At one point in class, on an intuitive hunch, I asked the students to close their eyes and raise their hands if anyone could say they completely loved themselves. I was surprised that no one raised their hands in a class of 35 people. I then threw away my curriculum for the night and spent the rest of class exploring why no one could say they loved themselves. A variety of reasons were given for why they couldn't love themselves; some pertained to religion, others to powerful messages from parents that told them how worthless and unlovable they were. Still others cited past love relationships that left their hearts in tatters and their self-esteem permanently damaged. I knew then that I would spend time over the next few weeks focusing on self-love, in the hope that it just might make a difference in my students' own healing and loving themselves.

Like I tell my students all the time, I'm no expert on love. I'm just a keen observer, forever the student, always curious about love and understanding it. The more I learn about love, the more humbled I've become, as I realize how little I really do know about love. But from my humble experience as a teacher and therapist in the field of human services, this is what I came up with and shared with my students about understanding self-love:

> Did you know that the average relationship in the United States, when you combine dating, marriage, and cohabitation, lasts about 4 months? That should tell you right there that whatever we're doing isn't working very well.
>
> Most people surveyed assume that love doesn't last and that it will disappoint you. Really, how jaded have we become? Are we not doomed from the start with an attitude like that?
>
> Leo Buscaglia used to ask his students in his love class, "If you could be you or you could be someone else, what would you choose?" Sadly, in asking this question of his students over the years, well over 80% answered that they would rather be someone else. The chances of replicating you in all your unique DNA is 1 in 73 trillion. Yet people would rather be someone else. To me, that is very sad and tragic, especially when you consider there will never be another you that ever walk this planet.
>
> So many of us focus so much on finding our "ideal" mate our "soul mate," when our focus should really be on becoming that ideal mate. But becoming that ideal mate starts with loving yourself. And how do you begin to love yourself?

## KNOW YOURSELF

The quest toward loving yourself begins with knowing who you are. How can you begin to know another when so few of us know ourselves? I think you need to ask yourself, "Who am I?" throughout your life. This simple question may be the most profound question you ever ask in your life. Hopefully, in answering the question, "Who am I," the answer will be much different at 46 years old than at 16 years old, and a whole lot different at 86 years old. Are you really the *you* of you, or are you the you that everyone has told you you are? Do you really know who you are?

I introduce students to a Zen-Buddhist exercise in which you ask yourself over and over like a mantra, the question, "Who am I?" Usually you start answering by all the roles you fulfill in your life; I'm a son, a daughter, a wife, a husband, a brother, a sister, a teacher, or a lawyer. Eventually when you run out of all your roles, the question takes you to a deeper, more profound place. After you lose all the roles, what's left of you?

If I had to create a perfect society, I might begin by requiring young people in their early 20s to spend a year living on their own and not in any romantic relationship. Of course this idea is not popular at all with any of my students. I think living on your own and not be in any relationship would force you to look within, and invite you to come to terms with who you really are.

When I was in graduate school, I had just broken off a long-term relationship and, through a self-imposed dating exile, I dated no one for a full year. Of course, that didn't go over well for the people in my life at the time; I was accused of being gay or just plain weird. My experience as a young male (which I don't think is a whole lot different for young females) was that I should be in relationship with someone, or I should at least be pursuing someone for a relationship, or I'd be labeled as gay. How sad is that?

My year in exile from dating turned out to be one of my best years of my life. I was freed from the cultural pressure of being in a relationship or pursuing a relationship. It freed me up to be a more authentic version of myself. There was no pressure to impress someone, to say, or do, or even wear the "right thing." I could just be Tom and not give a shit about what anyone else thought of me or what kind of an impression I was leaving. I was free to experiment and try different things in expanding my vision of myself.

Too many times I see young people living at home, and then they go from home right to college and they find themselves in a relationship right away that usually leads to them living together. Not too long after that, they end up marrying. There is no space to be with themselves alone and discover who they are beyond the context of a relationship. So I believe a fundamental part of loving yourself is knowing who you are beyond the context of a relationship.

e. e. cummings once stated, "The greatest battle you will ever fight in your life is the battle to be yourself. It is the only battle worth fighting." Too often, we live our lives never really finding ourselves within ourselves.

## MAKE A DECISION TO LOVE YOURSELF

I didn't make a decision to consciously love myself until my senior year at Burnsville High School. Up until that point, as I chronicled earlier, I had zero self-love. Then, during that year in Gramma's Social and Family Living class, I began to see for the first time the importance of loving myself. It all started with making a conscious decision to begin to love myself.

My life did not become any easier all of a sudden as I decided to love myself. But the act of making a conscious decision created a momentum in which I could live into the answer. For instance, I used to do a lot of self-deprecating—anything to get a joke and make people laugh. I would say such things as, "I've got a face for radio," or "I look really good from far away, like from a blimp." Deciding to love myself made me pause and really look at what I was saying about myself. I became more conscious of criticizing and belittling myself. I became much more aware of the words I used to describe myself, and I started changing my vocabulary regarding myself. I started making myself more of a priority. I refrained from labeling myself as "selfish" and instead started seeing what I did as an act of self-care, and that I was worth it.

## ACCEPT WHAT IS

Serenity Prayer
*God, grant me the serenity to accept the things I
cannot change, the courage to change the things I
can, and the wisdom to know the difference.*

For years, I could rail against God and my parents for having a crooked face and a birth defect left hand, but that would only leave me stuck, depressed, angry, and in a victim role. "Woe is Tom." I would just be stuck in my sorrow and pity. Blaming others would get me nowhere. At some point in my quest to love myself, I had to accept what is; my face and hand would always be this way, so what was I going to do about it?

I worked for 12 years as a therapist. I would say that a major cause of clients' need for therapy is a refusal to accept what is. I would see people who refused to accept a break up or a divorce. After hearing their stories, I would swear it just happened recently, only to find out the break up occurred months ago, or a year, or two, or even three years ago. But they would be stuck in their sorrow and pain because of a refusal to accept what is.

I've seen this refusal to accept what is with alcoholics who do not accept that they are alcoholics, with devastating results. Or people who refuse to believe they have been diagnosed with a bipolar condition, resulting in them going off their medications and causing dire harm (in some cases suicide) to themselves and those around them.

A place to start in loving yourself, then, is to accept what is. That which you cannot accept you cannot let go of. I may not be able to change my face or hand, but accepting what is got me out of the victim role and propelled me into beginning to empower myself. I was no longer stuck in the past. Acceptance of what is allowed me to focus on the present and the things about me that I could change. For instance, at the age of 16, I began to work out on a daily basis. That was something I had control over. Now, 39 years later, I went through a fitness test for my medical provider around my asthma, and I tested out at one of the highest fitness levels they had seen at that particular clinic for someone my age with asthma.

Accepting what was allowed me to shift my focus away from things I couldn't change and refocused me on what I could change. For instance, in my teen years, I began to focus on becoming a better version of myself; that has been a lifelong quest. I began to focus on improving my personality and my character. In doing that, I grew in my own self-confidence. I burst through my own shell of insecurity and began making changes in myself, and I saw myself more and more as a lovable human being. But this personal odyssey of coming to love myself began with the first step of accepting what is.

## FIND SOMEONE WHO BELIEVES IN YOU

Have you ever wondered why, if you take two kids who grow up in the same neighborhood, who essentially come from the same background, same poor neighborhood, same schools, same religion, same family type, and same culture, why one kid ends up growing up and going to prison and the other kid grows up to be a successful college professor? The answer is in resiliency studies.

What we know from resiliency studies is that usually the children who make it out of the ghetto, out of a bad situation, had someone beyond their parents who believed in them. That believer didn't have to be in the child's life more than a year, but that person came at a crucial time in the child's life, almost like a tipping point. That pivotal person could have been a coach, a social worker, an aunt, or a teacher, but the crucial piece is that the person believed in that child and demonstrated that belief.

That's why it became so important for me to meet Gramma when I was 17 and in my senior year of high school. She was the first person I ever met outside of my family who really believed in me. She saw my worth before I even knew it was there. She believed in me so strongly that for the first time, I began to believe in myself as well. Her belief in me began to lead me down the road of beginning to love myself.

This was brought home to me again as an instructor just this past year in one of my classes. Megan was one of my students in my Basic Counseling Skills class. A primary assignment in the class is to keep a journal. I spontaneously brought up her name in my class as an example of someone keeping an excellent journal (although I rarely single out a particular student)—how Megan put so much effort into writing her journal, really pouring her heart and soul into it. Then I quickly moved on with the class.

Sometime afterward, Megan came up to me and told me how much my words, my belief, meant to her. Apparently she came from a family in which she was constantly put down. She was constantly told that she wasn't going to amount to much and that she was wasting her time getting a human service degree, since it didn't pay much anyway. She told me that no other teacher had ever complimented her or believed in her before. She went on to thank me and a true bond was born.

The lesson I learned from that is how powerful my words and beliefs can be with my students. I no longer hold back; I tell my students all the time that I believe in them and encourage them. It is amazing to see them begin to awaken and believe in themselves. I tell them all the time, "I don't see your past. All I see is who you are and what you can become."

So I think that what really matters in loving ourselves is having someone in our lives who genuinely believes in who we really are.

**FORGIVE YOURSELF**

If you search online for "steps to loving yourself," you will see many other important steps that I don't include in here, such as self-affirmations, making yourself a priority , watching your self-talk, and so on. All of these are very important. Go into any Personal Growth section at a bookstore and you will see various books focusing on these various dimensions of self-love. But a step you will not often find listed, yet one that I think is essential in your journey of loving yourself, is forgiving yourself.

One of the kindest, gentlest, most loving things you can do for yourself is to forgive yourself. It is also one of the hardest things for us to do. It seems it is much easier to forgive others than to forgive ourselves. As a therapist, I saw this play out frequently with clients.

For example, I had one couple in which the wife committed an infidelity. They were in therapy to try to move through this in their relationship. After much work in therapy, the husband finally came to a point where he forgave his wife for her transgression. But the wife could never get to a point of forgiving herself. It was like a self-imposed penance. They ended up dropping out of therapy and I never did find out what happened to them.

By not forgiving yourself, you end up stuck in the past, unable to move forward. You end up living in a state of sadness, hurt, and guilt. Not forgiving yourself keeps you immobilized and frozen in time.

Forgiving yourself allows you to be free, to let go of that part of yourself that kept you imprisoned in your pain. A very important step in loving yourself and accepting who you are is to forgive yourself.

These steps in self-love had an impact on my students and they continue to have an impact on me. Each week we would explore yet another dimension of the topic of love. It was rarely me leading them; the class became much more of a collaborative adventure of sharing and mutual discovery. One student told me, about 4 weeks into the semester, when I discussed the possibility of scheduling a quiz for the next week, "I've learned nothing in regards to regurgitating facts and figures but I've learned so much more than I could have imagined about myself and loving who I am."

All too quickly, the semester was drawing to a close. Students protested that the course should meet more than once per week or that it should be a two semester class, not one. No one wanted it to end, including me. On the last days of class, students presented their "love projects." Their assignment was to be as creative as they wanted to be and present to the class on some dimension related to love. Most of the projects were quite good. For instance, some presented book reports on some aspect of love (I introduced this as a project possibility because I'm still in search of a text for this class). Others wrote poetry or songs and shared them with the class. In one particularly creative project, a student sent out 75 6"x 6" quilting squares to everyone she knew and asked them to write, with permanent, water resistant markers, something about what love means to them. In the quilt square she sent me, I wrote, "Love many and each the most." When she received all of the quilt squares, she sewed them together into what she called her "Love Quilt" and shared it with the class.

Two particular projects stood out to me as quite profound. The first involved a student who loved photography. She asked children under 10 years old, "What is love?" and "Do you love yourself?" In her presentation, next to their answers, she posted their pictures. The children's answers were so pure and innocent—and entertaining as well. For instance, they gave such answers as the following:

"I love myself because I'm me." (Age 6)

"I love myself because my mommy tucks me in every night, kisses me, and says I'm beautiful, and I believe her." (Age 5)

When asked, "What is love?" some of their answers were,

"When Mommy gives Daddy the best piece of chicken" (Age 5),

"Love is what's in the room with you at Christmas
if you stop opening up presents and listen" (Age 7).

Remarkably, when the next student presented, she had done the exact same project, except that instead of interviewing little kids, she had interviewed adults over 65 years old and asked the very same questions, "What is love?" and "Do you love yourself?" She also included their photos next to their responses. Notably, the little children's responses were not much different than the older adults'. For instance, one 75-year-old woman's response to the question, "Do you love yourself?" was, "After all these years, I've come to a place of really loving and accepting who I am for just being me. That seems like enough."

The similarity of the answers from the young children and the older adults made me pause in wonder and ask why these two groups seem to love and accept themselves so readily, and yet my classroom full of students from 18 to 55 years old have such difficulty in loving themselves that not one could raise a hand to my question earlier in the semester, "Do you love completely who you are?"

Something happens between 10 years old and 65 years old that makes loving ourselves such a challenge. The only answer I could come up with is this is that neither the young children nor the older adult group cares what others think about them. A young child still has yet to spend years of school being judged and evaluated by teachers and classmates, and hasn't come to a point yet where other people's opinions, beyond their parents, really matter.

Conversely, it seems, by the time you reach your elderly years, you've finally come to a place of comfort in your own skin, at which point people's opinions about you and what they think of you no longer matter. It's those in-between years during which we waste so much energy wondering about what others think of us, and how their opinions matter seems to get in the way of our own acceptance and love of ourselves.

Perhaps I'll have more of a handle on why this is after years of teaching my love class.

# Homeward Bound

*When I awoke this morning something inside of me told me this would be my day. I heard the morning train, I felt the wind change, too many times I'm on my way.*
*Come on sunshine, what can you show me? Where can you take me to make me understand? The wind can shake me, brothers forsake me, the rain can touch me, but can I touch the rain?*

*Then I got to thinking what makes you want to go to know the wherefore and the why. So many times now, oh Lord, I can't remember if it's September or July. . . .*

—Gordon Lightfoot, *"The Wherefore and the Why"*

*Men come tamely home at night only from the next field or street, where their household echoes haunt, and their life pines because it breathes its own breadth over again; their shadows morning and evening reach further than their daily steps. We should come home from afar, from adventures and perils, and discoveries every day with new experience and character.*

—Henry David Thoreau

> *To be free, to be able to stand up and leave everything behind-without looking back-to say YES.*

> —Dag Hammerskjold, *Markings*

Missouri has always been known as the Gateway to the West. It was my gateway to the east as I crossed from the 24th state, the start of the Pony Express, and the start of the Oregon Trail into Kentucky passing through Cairo, Illinois, before crossing both the Mississippi and Ohio rivers on my way in to Kentucky.

Kentucky was originally part of Virginia. It became the 15th state in 1792. It is known as the Blue Grass State, blue grass being prevalent in many of the pastures throughout the state. Kentucky has the distinction of having the highest per capita number of deer and turkey in the United States. It also has the nation's most productive coalfield. It is the only state in which three of its borders are rivers: the Ohio River to the north, the Mississippi River in the west, and the Big Sandy River in the east. Kentucky is known for horse racing, blue grass music, bourbon distilleries, tobacco, and college basketball.

Five years before I reached Kentucky, when my brother and two of his friends paddled their kayaks from the source of the Mississippi River in northern Minnesota to New Orleans, he had said that they knew they were in the South when they were camping outside a small town on the river in Kentucky. He had asked the population of the town. The guy replied, "Five hundred, including the coloreds."

I knew I was in the South when I ran across a slave block. It was near the middle of the state, in a small town. The slave block was at the edge of the downtown and it was basically a slab of uneven cement, nondescript, with a slight downward slope to it, about 4 feet long and a few feet wide. Part of it was obscured by an overgrown bush and the other side was in the shadows from a nearby building. I would have passed it completely except I was looking for a rest spot to rearrange my bike panniers, and this looked like a refuge from the hot noonday sun. I knew nothing of its significance until I was right on top of the block and saw the tarnished, weather-beaten, bronze plaque that said, "1000s of slaves were sold on this slave block."

After I read the plaque, I was stunned, and paused for a moment, feeling as if I was on some kind of holy ground. I became quiet and thought about the misery that took place on this spot. For instance, it was common during the slave trade for families to be split up, auctioned off, and sold like cattle, and for brothers and sisters never to see each other again. I could only imagine the anguished wailing that this slave block witnessed for it was not unusual when slaves were sold to break up families where siblings and parents would never see each other again. The cruelty is beyond words what we did to the slaves.

Years later, I taught a course on multicultural awareness. Our history with people of color in this country is not something to be proud of. For instance, one of the fastest ways for Europeans coming to America to assimilate and be accepted was to join in the common hatred of the black man. The "melting pot" mentality was open only to Euro Americans; people of color were seldom part of that melting pot philosophy, and so their assimilation into mainstream culture was never fully accepted.

It is no longer politically correct to be so blatant with our prejudice and discrimination, but make no mistake, it is still alive and well, just more subtle.

For example, one of my Somalia students, a woman with a strong accent who had been in the United States less than 7 years, reported to me about her calling about a townhome that she and her family were interested in buying. They were told that the last model had been sold. Skeptical, she had her Caucasian classmate with no accent call the same models 20 minutes later. She was welcomed with a friendly voice and encouraged to come down and visit because there were plenty of models still open.

In another incidence of racism a black sheriff from one of the counties outside of Minneapolis related the following incident that happened to him a few years back. He turned 45 years old, and his wife, sensing that her husband might be going through a midlife crisis, surprised him by getting him a brand new, candy apple red

Corvette. He was off duty traveling with a buddy of his who was also black. In a classic case of being in the "wrong place at the wrong time," they found themselves cruising in a white suburb. Soon he noticed that they were being followed by a couple of cops. Apparently the cops were quite suspicious of two black men traveling together in a new Corvette.

Finally, in the downtown area, the cops pulled them over at a stop light. Four squad cars surrounded them. With guns drawn, the officers put a spotlight on their vehicle. Soon, both men were pulled out of the car, face down, arms behind their backs, and hands cuffed. When the police asked for the sheriff's ID, he told them it was in his back pocket. They pulled out his wallet, opened it up, and saw his sheriff's badge; the next thing he heard was a collective, "Oh shit" from the arresting officers. This wasn't some isolated incident in a small, rural southern town in the 1920s; this happened today in a metropolitan area in Minnesota of over 3 million people. Incidents like this make me wonder just how far we've advanced from those long ago slave days.

I find my students frequently say they don't need a multicultural awareness course; "We're beyond that Tom, that kind of thing doesn't happen anymore." I call them the "post racism generation." However it's incidences like above that make me differ with their current, erroneous perceptions.

I find it particular appalling when I overhear students say about immigrants, "They should act more American." That usually is a coded expression for they should act more white. Too often in our history we have equated white as synonymous with human, for right. Students will moan and complain about Mexicans or other immigrants not knowing the language and I will hear them say things like, "If they are going to come here, they should speak English." Little do they know that immigrants coming to this country are learning English at a faster rate (about 2 years) than any other previous wave of immigration in our recorded history.

In my course today, students will be up in arms about affirmative action "giving people of color an unfair advantage." But in the end, students are well aware of the score. I ask them each semester how many of the Caucasian students would want to change places with people of color, since they seem to be getting such a "good deal." I've been asking this question each year I teach my multicultural awareness course, and not one white student has ever raised a hand.

As I left the slave block I noticed the further I pedaled toward the eastern seaboard, the more I noticed the sky became hazier. Because of the air pollution wafting in from the east, the mountains seemed to capture the hazy, polluted sky, and sunny, clear days became rarer.

Kentucky provided other contrasts to Minnesota. Minneapolis-St. Paul has working class suburbs followed by middle class suburbs, next to upper middle class, and finally rich suburbs. In Kentucky, it was not unusual to see a mansion at one end of the block followed by a shack at the other end of the same block. I was told this dated back to slave days, when the property included the owner's mansion at one end of the property and the servant quarters at the other end of the property.

After biking for about 1,000+ miles through relatively flat country, in eastern Kentucky I started seeing mountains again, as I approached the Appalachia region. Eastern Kentucky is home to coal mining. I began to see more and more coal trucks on the highway. It was now well in to July, and the humidity and temperatures hovered continually in triple digits. The air was thick with coal dust. It was not unusual, by the end of a long day of biking, to wipe the sweat off my face with my bandana and have streaks of black coal suttee left on the cloth.

By the time I reached the Virginia border and the Blue Ridge Mountains, I was invigorated. This would be the "bell lap," my last push to the sea. I felt like a race horse that had the finish line in sight. I was going to make it.

The state of Virginia was the first New World colony. It is known as the "mother of presidents." Eight different U.S. presidents were born in Virginia. Forests cover about 65% of the state. By the Civil War, 31% of the state was enslaved. During the height of the Civil

War, in 1863, 48 northern counties in the state separated to form the state of West Virginia, which pledged its loyalty to the Union.

Today, Virginia has the highest concentration of technology workers of any state. Computer chips became its highest grossing export in 2006, surpassing the traditional top exports of tobacco and coal combined.

You might say I was a bit cocky coming into Virginia. By this time, I had bicycled through the mighty Rocky Mountains and six other ranges topping over 11,000 feet. When I looked at the Blue Ridge topping out at between 6,000 and 7,000 feet, I thought it would be no problem, a piece of cake. I was dead wrong, and I accentuate the "dead" part. Virginia may have been the toughest state I biked in.

It didn't help that the derailleur on my bicycle wasn't working properly, so instead of having 21 speeds available to me, I was down to seven speeds. I did not have the expertise to fix it, nor the funds to get it repaired.

The topography of Virginia was different from the topography of the West. The Rocky Mountains had miles of gradual foothills to bike through and when I finally found myself ascending mountain passes, they were usually at a 5% to 6% grade. Bicycling through Virginia was like being on a continual roller coaster. There were no foothills. As soon as I got down one mountain, there was another staring me in the face, usually at a grade steeper than what I had ever encountered before; it was not unusual to see 7% or 8% grades, which doesn't sound like a big difference until you are on a bicycle with only seven speeds and you are hauling an additional 30 pounds of weight. Virginia was my last state and it kicked my butt!

Virginia is steeped in Civil War history. There were so many memorials and plaques commemorating some battle fought long ago that it felt as if I could throw a rock in any direction and hit a memorial! I do love history, but it would have taken me about week longer if I had stopped and read every memorial or visited every local museum. I didn't have the time, and I was running out of funds.

About 75 miles into Virginia, still in the middle of the Blue Ridge Mountains, I stayed overnight for free in what I would call a "flop house," at the intersection of my route and the famous Appalachian hiking trail that traverses the east coast from Georgia in to Maine. The house was in a rural setting, just a clearing in the woods. It was a very old, wooden, two-story home with a wraparound porch. It was dilapidated, in bad need of paint and repair. But I wasn't complaining. The bonus was that I could spend a night indoors, a rare luxurious treat and to top it off, it was free!

About a dozen people were spread out in rolled out sleeping bags, bunking down for the night. Some of them had their camp stoves fired up, cooking their dinner on the porch. There were clothes drying on an impromptu clothesline, a solitary rope strung across the back porch. I ran into three guys from Georgia, around 19 or 20 years old, who had been on the Appalachian Trail starting in Georgia a little over a month prior, and were planning to hike the whole route into Maine. They invited me to dinner, and I gladly accepted, since it was rare that I ever ate with anyone on the trip. Besides, I was looking forward to breaking bread with some people from the "Deep South." I was curious to hear about what life was like in a world I had never visited. I was also interested in hearing about traversing the Appalachian Trail, a hike I had heard about and had some interest in perhaps doing in the future. They were equally excited about meeting me, since I was a "northern boy" from Minnesota, and they were curious to hear more about my adventures traveling by bike from coast to coast.

We shared enthusiasm about the meal they were cooking that night—a healthy dose of black-eyed peas and smoked pork. I hadn't had a hot cooked dinner in over 2 months. I thought this would be a welcome change of pace to my usual peanut butter and jelly sandwiches.

Soon the meal was ready, the aroma intoxicating, and I had a big smile on my face as they filled up my bowl to the brim. They were all eagerly staring at me as I took my first heaping tablespoon full of peas and pork. I immediately just about gagged, as the taste was so uninviting and bland. "So, what do you think? Do you like it?" they asked. They smiled and nodded their heads, expecting enthusiastic validation for their culinary creation. It was all I could do to feign pleasure and gratitude for their meal. "Oh this is really good," I replied. I desperately wanted to spit it all out and pretend this never happened. Soon, after three or four bites of this deadly drivel, I noticed that all of a sudden, my peanut butter and jelly sandwiches didn't sound so bad after all.

Later, we swapped stories of adventure into the night. Before retiring for the evening, they asked me if I'd like to share in smoking their last "doobie" for the trip. I politely declined, and snuck back into my pack where I discreetly spread some peanut butter on a piece of bread and smuggled it in to my sleeping bag, where I later ate in quiet delight. They told me how bummed out they were; they had brought two pounds of pot they thought would last them the whole trip. Here they were, not even at the halfway point, and they were all out. The next morning, I said my goodbyes to the Georgia boys as I headed down the road humming the John Denver tune "Rocky Mountain High."

Finally, the unrelenting Blue Ridge was starting to lose its grip on my tortured body as it slowly receded in my rear-view mirror. I was entering the coastal plain of Virginia, where once again the terrain flattened out in anticipation of the ocean. The coast was no longer days or weeks away, it was now hours away. The thought of seeing the ocean again renewed my spirits, and seemed to quicken my pace.

Within 20 miles of the coast, I had to stop and pause and take it all in. I saw my first seagulls. I noticed the air smelled familiar but different. Then it dawned on me, I was beginning to smell the sea, an aroma I hadn't run into since I put my foot in the Pacific Ocean to start this trip almost 2 months earlier.

Soon, I came upon the famous Jamestown Settlement. I read all about the historical significance of the site. I found myself edgy and anxious as I strolled through the site. It's not often you run into the site of the first European settlement in the New World. Still, all I wanted to do was get back on my bike and ride for the coast.

My head was filled with daydreams as I clicked off 1 mile, then another, in my quest for the sea, a march of destiny. I wondered if I would bike right in, fully clothed, into the ocean, and I fantasized about a big marching band welcoming me, complete with reporters from NBC news eager to interview me, perhaps doing the talk show circuit later with Johnny Carson.

Now there were more and more seagulls in my midst, and the faint aroma of the sea was becoming more distinct and apparent. I pedaled upon the Yorktown battlefield memorial, but I quickly left, rationalizing that I could always stop back after my date with destiny and the sea.

On Sunday, July 16, 1981, I had been biking 52 days and including rest days, on the road 58 days. It was a rare sunny, blue-sky day on the east coast. The temperature was hovering at 100° as I dismounted my bike and began to slowly push it through the sand to the water's edge, the Atlantic Ocean. Hundreds of people were lounging on their blankets laid out on the sand, some napping, others listening to their boom boxes. To my left, young children made a sandcastle. To my right, teenagers tossed a Frisbee® back and forth. Up ahead, a woman played with her golden retriever while others swam in the surf. There was no banner or marching band welcoming me; no reporters either.

At 1:30 p.m., I arrived at the sea. I stayed there on the beach for the longest time, feeling the sand beneath me, closing my eyes trying to take it all in, listening to the seagulls above. I had actually done it. I had biked from sea to sea! It wouldn't really sink in until days later, when I regaled family and friends with stories and pictures from the trip. Once I arrived at this fairy tale destination, it was like a magnet that wouldn't let me go. I wanted to pitch a tent and stay there forever, basking in the sun, sand, and waves. But then, the reality of my dire financial situation broke the spell, and after a few hours of napping on the beach and people watching and taking pictures of my bike to mark the occasion, I mounted my bicycle and biked into Williamsburg.

Later that day, I stopped at the Greyhound Bus station to purchase my ticket home. Much to my surprise and disappointment, I had miscalculated and didn't have enough money to get home; I could only make it to South Bend, Indiana. I would have to have my parents wire me the rest of the money once I got to South Bend in order to get home. After purchasing my ticket, I had only $4.27 to my name.

During the trip, I used to fantasize about the big steak dinner and mounds of desserts I would eat as part of my celebratory feast for having made it. Instead, with the meager funds I had left, I stopped at a smorgasbord (I was determined to have one meal that did not involve plastic!) and ordered a bowl of soup and some crackers. That was my big celebration meal! The place was packed with people all around me. There were all these pasty white tourists, with their big pot bellies and heaping plates of steaks, mashed potatoes, and corn bread. I thought, if anyone deserved a big meal it was me, having biked 112 miles that day. Instead, I headed back to a new construction site, ate the last of my peanut butter and jelly, and called it a night.

Early the next day, I biked the 12 miles into town, found a bicycle box at the local bike dealer, took apart my bike, packed it up, and hopped the Greyhound home. I had been on a cross-country Greyhound trip only once before, from Denver to Minneapolis on New Year's Eve. In Denver, I knew I was in for an adventure when the trip started. As the bus driver announced the list of don'ts, and got to the part about illegal drugs, everybody behind me started laughing. I took the only seat left, next to an old man in white hair that had his headphones on and a neat stack of 20 magazines and newspapers piled up in front of him; there would be no idle chit chat with this old curmudgeon. Later in the night, the bus was actually pulled over outside of Lincoln, Nebraska, for speeding. I had never heard of a Greyhound pulled over for speeding!

I figured there would be nobody at the bus station at Omaha when we pulled in right at midnight on New Year's Eve; I was wrong. It looked like a weirdo convention as I stepped off the bus into a crowd of people. Within a matter of minutes, a tall man with silver hair in a trench coat approached and propositioned me. I was stunned, thinking, "What are the odds that I run in to something like this?" I made up a feeble excuse like, "Sorry, but my bus is coming any minute now," as I escaped into the crowd, hoping I'd never see the man again.

Thankfully, my trip home from Virginia on this Greyhound was uneventful. I remember how luxurious the bus felt; there were padded, cushy seats that I could adjust. After spending thousands of miles torturing my rear end on a Spartan-like bike seat, I was in the lap of luxury. There was even air conditioning! Most of the time, I stared out the window, amazed at how quickly the miles slipped by; distances that would take days and weeks to cover on my bike took only minutes or hours.

The total distance I covered on the bike trip was 3,980 miles. The trip took me 59 days with a total of 7 rest days. I averaged 90.5 miles per day on my bike. I averaged 85 miles per day until Pueblo, Colorado; after Pueblo, when I was finally in shape and out of the mountains, I increased my average considerably to 110.3 miles per day. There were 13 days that I bicycled over 100 miles. I had nine flats, six broken spokes, one replaced chain, and one sore ass!

It's been a little over 30 years since I completed my bicycle odyssey across America. I have always kept a journal, since I was 17 years old, and still have all the journals across my life except one—the one I kept on my bicycle trip. It would be the longest trip alone with my thoughts that I had ever gone on, and consequently, my journal became a familiar friend to which I would pour out my heart and soul each evening before sleep writing page after page about my daily adventures. It was the only witness to my journey.

Today, I rarely talk about my bike trip to anyone. I found out early on, when people would ask, "So tell me about your trip. How was it?" that people really only wanted a convenient sound bite like, "Oh, it was great," or "It sure was beautiful." I found myself frustrated in trying to encapsulate the journey of my soul into a few words that people could digest and take in. Soon, I didn't bother; I kept the memories close to my soul.

Over the years, in the quiet recesses of my heart, I often pondered, "Why did I go on the trip anyway? How did it make a difference in my life?" For many years, I had no answer. Oh, I knew I had done it partly in response to a high need for adventure, built into my DNA, I suppose. Remember, I had a grandfather who went West on a covered wagon, a father who survived Pearl Harbor and 63 bomber missions in WWII, and a brother who paddled the length of the Mississippi River.

Certainly this quote from my journal near the end of my trip said a lot about what the trip was like for me:

7/12/81 Berea, Kentucky

> One thing I'm learning each day and will carry with me is the lesson of perseverance. Remember well, Tom, all the days you biked 'til utter fatigue would set in, only to rise the next morning to do it all again.
>
> Remember all the times your tent leaked and left you with a soggy sleeping bag, or the times you were caught in downpours soaking yourself and your belongings.
>
> Remember all the times maps and guidebooks listed cafes and grocery stores, only to arrive and find them closed or no longer in business, leaving you with a parched thirst and a large hunger.
>
> Remember well all the times your body begged for mercy as you biked up what seemed like never-ending mountain passes. Remember as well the times that it snowed and sleeted so hard that you could barely

open your eyes as you pedaled into near white-out conditions above the tree line.

Remember all those sleepless nights when you were harassed by local town folk. Remember well the heat and humidity that would sap you of your strength and leave your spirit drooping.

Finally, remember all the times you wrestled with the thought of quitting, only to move past it and ride your bike another day.

Don't let this journey be an isolated experience, put up on a shelf and categorized, never assimilated within your everyday life. Instead, take the lessons you have learned from this journey, and apply them to your life, so that you may live life more fully and avoid the greatest disease of our time: complacency.

Today, I would answer that the mind knows fewer inhibitions than the body. The trip was more challenging mentally than physically. Many times, I wanted to quit, but my mind pushed on. It was a great lesson in perseverance and determination. I suppose the trip really helped to empower my soul. There is very little I fear now, and I think nothing is out of my reach. There is very little that intimidates me. Before when I saw limits; now I only see opportunity.

# Epilogue

I lost my journal of the trip within a month of getting back home. Losing it was like losing a best friend; I had poured myself so completely into those pages, and then I lost them. On some level, I suppose that writing this book was a way to recover what was lost when I lost my journal.

Seven years later, during my honeymoon, I pulled into the hotel parking garage and forgot for a moment that my bike was attached to the roof of my vehicle. Much to my horror, my bike, Rocinante, named after Don Quixote's horse, was severed in half, making it completely unrideable.

As the years slipped by, often my new bicycle sat in my garage, gathering dust, rarely taken out for a ride. Then, in 1998, after I lost my marriage and my boys, I was granted a sabbatical from my college, and hooked up with a friend to bicycle across Canada's smallest province, Prince Edward Island. After dropping off my friend at the airport in Portland, Maine, I went back to ride through the Cape Breton Highlands of Nova Scotia, where I was caught in a Force 10 storm off the Atlantic. It was a nice idea to bicycle through the fall colors, but not during a storm that ravaged the coast and anything not tied down. For a number of years afterward, my bicycle lay idle in my garage except for the occasional 10-, 20-, or 30-mile ride.

Then in 2009, I decided to commemorate my 50th year on the planet by going for another epic ride on my bicycle. For years when I lived in Canada, I would drive through Banff and Jasper National Parks. I would look with envy at bicyclists traveling the park highway. The shoulders were wide and expansive, and the scenery in the parks held some of the most beautiful sites in the world, as evidenced by the great number of tourists who frequented the parks each year. I decided I would take the train from St. Paul to the east entrance of Glacier National Park, then bike up the Highway to the Sun through the park before heading north up to Canada, going through both Banff and Jasper National Parks. Finally, I would cut across British Columbia and then head south to Spokane, Washington, before catching the train back to St. Paul. All told, it would be a 26-day trip that would cover over 1,300 miles.

Banff is located on the western border of Alberta, next to British Columbia. It is Canada's oldest national park, established in 1885. The park encompasses 2,564 square miles, and is home to 56 different mammal species including grizzly, cougar, and caribou. It is one of the world's most visited national parks, averaging over 5 million visitors a year.

It is hard to describe what I saw in Banff. To say words like *beautiful, awesome, amazing,* or *spectacular,* seems in some way limiting of the experience. Biking through Banff and Jasper is like biking in an odyssey of wonder.

In passing from Banff to Jasper National Park, I rode past the Columbian Ice Fields. The ice fields cover 325 square kilometers, about the size of Vancouver. It's thought to be the most unique attraction in the Canadian Rockies. From the highway, visitors can see over 100 glaciers, ranging in thickness from 300 to 360 meters, made up of snow up to 400 years old. Of the eight major glaciers, the most prominent is Athabasca. Some of the highest mountains of the Canadian Rockies line its edges.

*Tired and lonely,*
*So tired*
*The heart aches*
*Melt water trickles*
*Down the rocks*
*The fingers are numb,*
*The knees tremble,*
*It is now,*
*Now that you must not give in.*

*On the path of others*
*Are resting places,*
*Places in the sun*
*Where they can meet.*
*But this*
*Is your path*
*And it is now,*
*Now that you must not fail.*

*Weep if you can,*
*Weep,*
*But do not complain.*
*The way chose you –*
*And you must be thankful.*

By Dag Hammarskjold, in the book *Markings*

In order to get to the Columbian Ice Fields and into Jasper National Park, I had to climb the famous Sunwapta Pass, which means "turbulent water" in Stoney Indian language. I heard of Sunwapta Pass the first day of my trip, when I ran into a bicyclist traveling from Portland, Oregon, to Portland, Maine. When I told her I would be going in that direction, she shuddered at the thought, telling me, "Oh yeah, I remember that pass. I went up it about 20 years ago. I'll never forget how it whipped my butt. That was one hell of climb. Good luck on that one!"

I remembered her words when I glimpsed my first sight of the pass far in the distance. Just then I felt a knot form in my stomach, knowing full well what was ahead of me, having climbed numerous mountain passes when I had traversed the United States 28 years before. Just to get to the pass, there is a 5,000 foot climb in elevation from Lake Louise in Banff to the beginning of the pass. Sunwapta is on the border of Banff and Jasper. Lake Louise is 76 miles south and the Jasper town site is 67 miles to the north. The pass was discovered in 1896, when Walter Wilcox and Robert Barret were on their way to explore the Columbian Ice Fields to the north, the largest ice fields in the world outside of the Arctic.

I spent the next 2 hours climbing, with a 100-pound trailer attached to my bike, inching my way to the top. I refused to pull into the periodic rest stops for cars, knowing that if stopped, my muscles would rapidly stiffen up, making an almost insurmountable task impossible.

My personal mantra, which I kept repeating to myself all the way up, was, "I am relentless!" I had to be relentless and have the "Eye of the Tiger" to make it up the pass. My speedometer was registering about 2 mph as each mile slowly ticked by. The muscles in my legs quivered and twitched under the strain, as sweat spilled like an open faucet down my face, saturating my clothes. I pedaled into the misery and pain; each foot of elevation levied an exacting a toll on my body. But with some strange, demented pride, I did not want to stop and have to walk my bike up the pass. I would feel defeated. Hauling a 100-pound trailer on foot up a pass is no easy task, either.

My body begged for mercy, pleading to stop this exercise in misery, but my mind would not give in. You know it is a tough climb when you see cars parked at rest areas over on the side with their hoods up, as their engines overheated from the strain. At one point as I passed a rest area, two guys looked at me in disbelief as they watched me slowly pulling my load up the pass. "Man that is some serious shit there! He is carrying the mother load," they said as I passed by. I was too strained to even acknowledge them or offer a perfunctory, "Hello." Finally, mercifully, the terrain ever so slowly started to flatten out, as I could see the Columbian Ice Fields loom in the foreground. That was the toughest pass I have ever climbed.

The next day, I bicycled into the Jasper town site, where I rendezvoused with my old friend, Fraser. We spent a few days hiking around the park and catching up on times gone by. Then I was on to British Columbia.

When I was planning the trip, I knew I would be passing through the town where my ex-wife and the boys lived in Alberta, but I was told by my ex-mother-in-law Mary Ellen that when I would be passing through, my ex and her husband and boys would be out of town on holiday. The best thing that came out of my marriage was my relationship with Mary Ellen. She would become my "Canadian mom," and I would become like a third son to her. I hadn't seen her in almost 5 years, and she was now living in a one bedroom apartment only a few miles away from her daughter and grandsons. She insisted when she found out that I was passing through that I stay with her for a couple of days; that, I was willing to do.

While I was there I found out that Mona and the boys were in town; something had come up to delay their holiday. That morning, while sharing breakfast with Mary Ellen in her apartment, the phone rang and this is what transpired, as recorded in my journal:

### *Thursday, July 23rd: Lost Lake Provincial Park, Alberta – Reflections upon seeing the boys*

*I saw the boys yesterday, 9 yrs after I said goodbye. I wasn't expecting to see them at all (Mona, Nick, and the boys were supposed to be away on holiday). Mona called Mary Ellen in the morning while we were eating breakfast, and wanted to know if I wanted to see the boys. I didn't know what to do, so I told Mary Ellen that we would call her back when I figured out what I wanted to do.*

*I was paralyzed with indecision. Such a simple request: "Do you want to see the boys?" Seven words that froze me; seven words I was not expecting to hear. So, now what do I do? I was glad Mary Ellen was there so I could process things out loud with someone who knew the situation at the time better than anyone else I know in the world.*

*For Mona, it seemed like no big deal, a simple offer. For me, it was a big deal! It seems like she had no clue what this meant to me.*

*Suddenly, I was awash in unexpected memories of the boys, so many of them so painful.*

*Questions started popping up: How would I handle seeing them after all of this time? Would I rush up and* grab them and hold them tightly? Would they have any sense of who I am? How would I be introduced? Would I be able to keep it together, or by just seeing them would I lose all composure and fall apart in a pool of tears? What would I say to them after all of this time? "Hi, I'm your first dad. I was the one that first helped usher you in to the world. I was kept out of your life by your mother and father . . . . " No, I didn't think that would work.

If I chose not to see them, would I regret it? If I did see them, would it set me back? Would it trigger so much pain and anguish within me that it would take years to relieve? Why do I have to face this shit?

Mary Ellen said it was a no-win situation; if I saw them, it couldn't help but bring forward painful memories, memories of what took place and what might have been. If I didn't see them, I would be riddled with the guilt of a missed opportunity, of what might have been. I agreed with Mary Ellen; no matter what way I chose, pain would be a part of the equation. In therapy, we call this being in a double bind, more commonly referred to as "damned if I do, damned if I don't."

I decided, after considerable angst and reflection, I would go ahead and see the boys. I think what pushed me over in that direction was that Mona had indicated to her mom that the boys wanted to meet me; they had been told I was Mona's first husband.

I decided to meet them, but only for a short period of time. There had to be boundaries to this encounter. If it was open-ended, I thought I might feel too much anxiety. I wanted Mary Ellen there as well, to be a witness, to be my support.

Tears came to my eyes unexpectedly as I processed this of all with Mary Ellen. I wasn't ready for this; once again, Mona caught me off guard.

It was agreed we would all meet for ice cream. I found myself pensive, anxious, and nervous as we drove off to *meet them. It didn't help that Mary Ellen missed the exit and we had to double back to meet them. The car ride there was pretty quiet.*

*Soon enough, all too soon, I was standing there before them, as they were sitting with their mom, finishing their burgers. I knew who was who right away. The boys were so tall, taller than their grandma; these were not the little boys I had left all those years back.*

*I was formally introduced by Mona to the boys: "Kelly and Ryan, this is Tom." My immediate reaction was to want to yell out, "Fuck, this sucks." How weird was this, to be formally introduced as some stranger to my boys? I named them. I was there at their birth, not their biological father. I cut their umbilical cords. I wrote their baptismal ceremony. I changed their diapers. I bathed them. I cuddled them when they cried. I fell asleep with them in the night. I stayed up with them when they were sick. I took them to daycare. I fought in the courts for over a year to be in their lives. And now, after all of that, after all of this time, I'm introduced as "Tom." They said, "I'm pleased to meet you, Tom," as they shook my hand, and they had no fucking clue who I am, or what role I played early on in their lives, outside of a few faded photographs of me in a long-forgotten photo album of their mother's. No, I was not ready for this. I fought the urge to run away and pretend this never happened. Instead I stayed. I had to see how it played out in front of me.*

*It felt as if I were dancing to a song I'd never heard before. The beat was peculiar and, try as I may, I couldn't pick it up. I stumbled.*

*There was so much to be said in the moment, yet few words came to my mouth. The whole thing felt surreal. Was this all really happening? Was this a dream, or a nightmare, or was it both? Meanwhile, I could feel a slight whisper inside of me saying, "Find the gift in all of this, Tom."*

*The scene suddenly shifted when the boy's father, Nick, appeared in order to switch cars with Mona. Why did he come now? Couldn't this wait for later? His hair was shorter on the sides now; he was bald on top and wore glasses. He looked like he had gained weight since I saw him last. I stood up to shake his hand and cracked a joke about his having a second career as a roofer, but he did not laugh. Instead, he barely shook my hand, barely acknowledged that I was even there. As soon as he appeared, he was gone.*

*I felt a rage well up as I grew indignant with the way he treated me. "How dare you treat me like shit," I thought to myself. More than anything, I wanted to go and beat the shit out of him, make him feel some pain, and give him a piece of my mind.*

*The boys were clearly tired, having been up since 5:30 a.m. helping their dad reroof their house. Neither was very present in the moment after eating a meal, being outside in the hot sun, and feeling tired from all the physical labor of the morning. This was one conversation I could not carry, nor did I want to. I, too, felt drained, but it was not from anything physical. I found myself listening a lot as Mona and her mom directed the conversation. Mostly, we talked about soccer and skiing, both things the boys clearly enjoyed. For some reason, I found myself wishing I had a soccer ball; I would much rather have played with them then have a semi-conscious conversation that neither would probably ever remember nor cherish. Neither looked very excited to be there or to meet me.*

*Soon, they were getting ready to say their goodbyes and go. I didn't want them to leave, but I didn't want them to stay either. In the end, all I could do was hug them, take a few pictures, and watch them drive away with their mother.*

*I'm glad I saw the boys, but I'm not sure why. Just then, the thought occurred to me, will I ever see them again?*

# About the Author

Since his cross-country bicycle trip across the United States, Tom has embarked on periodic bike trips through Prince Edward Island, Nova Scotia, and Glacier, Banff, and Jasper National Parks. He still has an adventure or two left on his bike.

Tom was born in Chicago, Illinois and grew up in the Minneapolis-St. Paul area. He grew up with a birth defect left hand and a paralysis of the right side of his face. He is the youngest of four children.

He has a master's degree in social work from the University of Georgia and an additional master's degree in marriage and family therapist from Kansas State University.

He has taught over 5,000 students in two countries (Canada and the United States) at the graduate, undergraduate, and community college levels in his 22-year teaching career. He is proud of being a dual citizen of Canada and the United States. He won Teacher of the Year in 2008 at his present college (Inver Hills Community College) and in 2012 won Education Minnesota's Human Rights Award for the state of Minnesota.

In addition to teaching, Tom also worked as a therapist for 12 years in in-patient, outpatient, and private practice settings. His clinical expertise was in loss and grief issues.

Tom never seems to get away from teaching, as he has spent the past 12 winters teaching over 3,000 students how to cross-country ski in both Washington state and Minnesota. He is a Professional Ski Instructor of America or (PSIA-Level 1, Nordic). His motto is, "Ski season never ends, it just changes form," as he loves to roller ski in those other seasons besides winter.

In the summer, he takes great joy in sailing his 14-foot Laser® sailboat called, "Living the Dream."

He currently resides in Inver Grove Heights, Minnesota.

| Trademark or registered trademark |
| --- |
| 7-Eleven® is a registered trademark of 7-Eleven, Inc. |
| Cheerios® is a registered trademark of General Mills, Inc. |
| Darth Vader™ is a trademark of LUCASFILM ENTERTAINMENT COMPANY LTD., Lucas Licensing Ltd., and Lucasfilm Ltd. |
| Frisbee® is a registered trademark of © 2004 *Wham-O,* Inc. |
| G.I. Joe™ is a trademark of Hasbro, Inc. |
| Google™ is a trademark of Google Inc. |
| Laser® is a registered trademark of Karaya (Jersey) Limited but also the subject of pending litigation at time of press. |
| Luke Skywalker™ is a trademark of LUCASFILM ENTERTAINMENT COMPANY LTD., Lucas Licensing Ltd., and Lucasfilm Ltd. |
| Perkins® is a registered trademark of Perkins & Marie Callender's, LLC and it affiliates. |
| Tyvek® is a registered trademark of E.I. du Pont de Nemours and Company. |
| |

CPSIA information can be obtained at www.ICGtesting.com
Printed in the USA
LVOW11s1834080914

403037LV00002B/438/P